Flexible Working

2nd edition

John Stredwick is a senior lecturer in Human Resource Management at Luton Business School. Before joining the school he spent 20 years as a personnel practitioner in a variety of industries.

Steve Ellis works in the financial services sector as a learning and development consultant specialising in flexible working and knowledge management.

The Chartered Institute of Personnel and Development is the
leading publisher of books and reports for personnel and
training professionals, students and all those concerned with
the effective management and development of people at
work. For details of all our titles, please contact the
publishing department:

tel: 020 8612 6204

e-mail publish@cipd.co.uk

The catalogue of all CIPD titles can be viewed on the CIPD website:

www.cipd.co.uk/bookstore

Flexible Working

2nd edition

John Stredwick
Steve Ellis

Chartered Institute of Personnel and Development

Published by the Chartered Institute of Personnel and Development

151 The Broadway, London SW19 1JQ

This edition published 2005
First published 1998

Typeset by Curran Publishing Services, Norwich

Printed in Great Britain by
The Cromwell Press, Trowbridge, Wiltshire

British Library Cataloguing in Publication Data

A catalogue of this manual is available from the British Library

ISBN 1-84398-055-X

Chartered Institute of Personnel and Development,
151 The Broadway, London, SW19 1JQ

Tel: 020 8612 6200

E-mail: cipd@cipd.co.uk   Website: www.cipd.co.uk

Incorporated by Royal Charter. Registered Charity No. 1079797

Contents

Figures and tables

Figures

Tables

Acknowledgements

The authors would like to acknowledge the help from numerous people and organisations in researching and writing this text. These are too numerous to list in full but special mention should be made of the following:

Dr Ted Johns, who provided a large number of sources and suggestions for development since the first edition.

Martyn Laycock, Geoff Joles, Kathy Whymark and Dawn Cooper for providing insights from their own experiences of flexible working.

Kevin White from Working Time Solutions and Bernard Murphy from Gleneagles Hotel for their kind assistance in the field of Annualised Hours.

Deborah Carre from Surrey County Council, Zoe Schoenfeld from Manpower UK Ltd and the staff of Work Life Balance Consultancy and 3M Ltd for their time and effort in providing case study material.

Finally to Stephen Partridge for his continuous advice and help as editor for the project.

About the authors

Steve Ellis lives in the UK but has worked in 11 countries consulting for one of the world's largest financial institutions since 1999, joining them from academia as a specialist in management and OD.

In 2005 Steve will complete his PhD in strategic knowledge-based working as part of a long-term research programme under the supervision of the University of Bradford, England.

He has co-authored textbooks in the fields of organisational behaviour and is also the author of *Knowledge based working, guidance for intelligent organisations* (2005)

In 2004 Steve founded a web-based guidance service, www.knowledge doctor.com, to provide guidance for executives struggling with the knowledge age. In this way Steve has been able to convert his experience and research findings into practical applications for executives who both need and value his advice. Steve presents regularly at KM conferences, and conducts seminars at the LSE and other business schools around the world. He spoke at the launch of the London Knowledge Network. He is also a member of the British Standards Knowledge Committee responsible for writing and publishing universal standards.

Dr John Stredwick is an academic and consultant in the fields of flexible working practices and reward and compensation. He has published widely on both these subject areas including six books and numerous articles. After 25 years as a human resources practitioner in manufacturing and service industries, he joined Luton Business School in 1992 and has since managed CIPD and Reward programmes.

He has been a keynote speaker at UK and international conferences and has regularly taught in Singapore and Dubai, while his books have been translated into Russian, Chinese and Polish. His expertise in reward issues has led to the commission to write flexible learning materials for Employee Reward modules on the CIPD professional development scheme.

Introduction

We are about half way through one of the great transformations of the world – a transformation in which centuries are compressed into decades. This transformation is from a society in which the financial and physical capital has been the dominant business resource to one in which the dominant resource will be knowledge.

(Drucker 1998, p124)

This quote provides a backdrop to this book. An issue of great concern to many academics, researchers and practitioners is the way organisations now use or abuse flexible working practices to ensure that their primary asset, intellectual and social capital – otherwise known as knowledge – is utilised effectively.

According to Patricia Hewitt, the UK Secretary of State for Trade and Industry, writing in 2003, the last decade has seen a revolution in the workplace. With female employees now constituting almost half of the workforce, the relationship between work and family life has altered dramatically, and the world of work needs to catch up.

Allowing people to work in ways that enable them to balance earning a living sensibly with all the other demands on their time is good not just for them but for their families and business too.

More and more enlightened companies, big and small, across a range of sectors are already enjoying the benefits of moving to a modern approach to flexibility. However according to the Minister there are still too many UK organisations where the old-fashioned long-hours culture prevails, and the costs of this are high. A survey completed recently by Peter Nolan of the Economic and Social Research Council (Nolan 2001) suggested that in the UK, 10 per cent of women and one-third of men consistently work over 50 hours per week. In the same survey the proportion of men satisfied with their working hours has fallen from 35 per cent 10 years ago to 20 per cent now. For women the fall is even more dramatic, with only 26 per cent reporting that they are satisfied, compared with 54 per cent 10 years ago.

Although the British work the longest hours in Europe, British levels of productivity are lower than in many other countries, and the loss of working time through stress costs British business over £12 billion per year.

The UK government has made it clear that it supports the move to more flexible working practices, and has announced a range of measures to encourage the transition.

Surrey County Council adopted wide-ranging flexible working practices as long ago as 1998. The wide variety of flexible working practices that the council supports includes:

- annual hours arrangements to cover for peaks and troughs of activity
- seasonal hours to cover tourism requirements
- term-time hours/school-time hours
- compressed working time to allow staff to work a nine-day fortnight
- team rotas to cover service needs and staff preferences
- part-time working with benefits and leave pro rata
- job sharing to mix the hours or skills of more than one employee in one job role.

The results of their policies included:

- cutting the number of offices used from 74 to 21
- trimming the number of workstations maintained by 20 per cent through increased use of job-sharing and hot-desking[1]
- reducing the space required per person by 33 per cent.

Under the council's 'Workstyle' initiative, some 3,500 staff will be affected, and a net capital expenditure saving of £6 million is expected (Bibby 2000).

The journal *Employment Trends* (April 2004) reported that Centrica, an essential services provider in the UK, is planning to increase the flexible working options open to its staff. The company has over a third of its UK workforce currently working some of the time at or from home. For Centrica the big drivers for increased flexibility are:

- seeking to become an employer of choice in tight labour markets
- improving retention of good employees
- opening up the pool of labour to include those cannot work to traditional patterns
- improving corporate performance on the diversity agenda.

THE FLEXIBLE WORKING WORLD

According to survey work conducted by Peter Nolan of the University of Leeds, director of the Economic and Social Research Council Future of Work programme (Nolan 2001), 70 per cent of senior professionals and managers now use the internet as part of their work.

When, in 1999, 15-year-old US schoolboy Jonathan Lebed used unfettered Internet access to make share deals in his bedroom at a profit of US$800,000 in less than a year, he became the first and only minor charged by the US Stock Exchange Commission with stock market fraud (Lewis 2001). He was stretching the concept of flexible working beyond normal boundaries, but he had created a clear and significant precedent. He had shown that traditional barriers to working and professional knowledge were no longer tenable.

One result of how both society and work is developing is that we can now clearly identify 'knowledge workers', who are ideally placed to take advantage of the opportunities offered by flexible working. That flexible working requires a very different approach to human resource management is now becoming apparent. The challenges and opportunities presented by this type of convulsion within society are on such a scale that estimates of what changes in the parameters of life, work and society will emerge are very hard to make.

Cowey (2000), Davenport and Prussak (1998) and Winter (1987) all report that the flexible working revolution has major implications for the way we live, work, socialise and interact with others in society.

THE ADVANTAGES, CHALLENGES AND RISKS OF FLEXIBLE WORKING

The move to increased flexibility offers some significant advantages to many businesses. Capitalising on the 24-hour economy often requires services to be provided when customers want them, not just when it is convenient to the provider. Dealing with peaks and troughs of demand becomes more manageable, and access is opened up to new labour markets where traditional working patterns cannot be contemplated.

Flexible working can also stimulate higher job satisfaction and commitment levels from employees, where they can see a clear personal benefit from the change. All the people spoken to in the research for this book who were actual flexible workers made it clear that they felt they achieved far more in flexible mode than they ever did before as nine-to-five-ers. They also had no desire ever to go back to traditional working patterns.

Alongside these advantages, flexible working also brings significant challenge. Organisations may need to rethink many aspects of their HR practices, for example to enable flexibilisation of rewards, and bring in new systems of monitoring and performance management.

There are risks involved with introducing flexible working, and these need not be understated. Risks resulting from a lack of standardisation over what is going on in the business might include allegations of unfair treatment by some sections of the workforce where flexibilisation is more readily adopted than others. Another risk may occur with the loss of managerial control and over-reliance on employees to become 'self-managed' where previously they were closely monitored. All of the challenges, advantages and risks will be covered in detail in this book.

A FURTHER CONSEQUENCE OF FLEXIBLE WORKING: SHRINKING TIME FRAMES

Once customers become accustomed to 'online' instant access, 24 hours and seven days a week, it becomes the norm and organisations that cannot replicate this are vulnerable.

HR and other managers now live in the midst of the turbulent tornado of the Internet, which has touched down and is tearing up previously accepted realities. Results have to be delivered often against very short time horizons. An appropriate example is an employee who asks for permission to work flexibly (which has been a right in the UK since the legislation of 2003). How long should he or she expect to wait for a response? Our experience suggests that in order to answer the request effectively, the organisation needs to have thought this through pretty clearly prior to getting the request. If the request is delivered to an organisation with no clear policies or thinking on what types of flexible working will and will not be sanctioned, that employee could be kept waiting weeks, if not months, for the answer.

Where clear guidelines and the practical implications of flexibility have been considered in anticipation of the requests, responses should be made in hours or days. On a broader level, flexible working practices as detailed in the following pages will often give managers an effective short cut to counter the new time pressure.

When New College Oxford was built in 1386, the building benefactor (the then Lord Chancellor) requested that acorns be planted in the college grounds, to become eventual replacements for the giant oak beams used in construction. Sure enough, these new beams were ready for replacing the old ones at the end of the nineteenth century. This type of forward thinking act only makes sense if tomorrow is an extension of today. Such acts contain a powerful belief that values are reasonably constant and will endure. In addition, such long-term thinking also displays a selfless attitude: if you plant an acorn, the benefit will accrue to others in the future. Contrast this tale of safe predictability with the effort of T-Mobile, a leading mobile telecommunications company which prides itself on being able to operate in a world where a new mobile telephone has to be designed, produced, tested, marketed and made obsolete within 6 months.

Similarly, Cisco Systems has long been famous for refusing to contemplate any project with a life-span of more than six months. That is not to say it does not do anything that takes longer than six months, but it frames all projects in such way that the six-month timeframe is the horizon. This approach not only builds in flexibility, but recognises that the world is moving so fast that what seemed like a winning idea at the beginning of the year might by June have become a lame duck.

DOES FLEXIBLE WORKING REQUIRE A NEW TYPE OF HR SERVICE?

Much traditional HR and management practice, from its Taylorist roots onwards, has focused on controlling activity through codification, enabling ease of replication. Ritzer (1996) noted a late twentieth-century form of Taylorism, the sociological phenomenon he named 'McDonaldis-ation', in which virtually any application of human behaviour can be reduced to essential, codifiable knowledge chunks. But what both Taylorism and McDonaldisation share is a paradigm where the HR manager's primary role is to ensure compliance and conformity. Para-doxically both logic and history suggest that new knowledge develop-ment and innovation will thrive not under conditions of control and enforced conformity, but under flexibility. This contradiction will remain uncomfortable unless a new definition of what constitutes good HR management can be constructed.

The reduction of HR management into written manuals has historically enabled organisations to manage people more efficiently. But such a practice is viable only where practices are relatively stable, and change is predictable. For the introduction of increased flexibility, many traditional tools and systems of management are not adequate.

The manager (HR or otherwise) who develops 'softer-edged' skills of relationship building, visioning, networking and team-enabling is far more likely to enhance performance than the manager who ensures conformity and adherence to procedure. In a crowded market place the ability to manage this differentiation and not just enforce conformity could be the way to sustained high performance.

There is another aspect, requiring change of a higher order of magnitude. Many traditional organisations were just not configured for flexible working. Established structures are designed for logical, predictable 'nine to five' chunks, but flexible working is simply not like that. In order to capture the innovative, creative energy of predominantly knowledge workers, organisations will need to become flexible places where innovation happens, where creativity is the norm not the exception, and employees are willing to share much more of themselves, their talents, aspirations and views than is currently achieved. This book is aimed at helping those seeking to operate more flexibly to achieve their aims.

FINDING YOUR WAY AROUND THE BOOK

We cover a wide area in this book, as the contents page indicates, and you may want a little more guidance on where to look for your special interests.

If you are interested in flexibility from the employee's viewpoint, then look in Chapter 1, which has a number of individual case studies and provides some guidance on work–life balance issues. You will find more about the specifics of work–life balance and examples of organisational approaches to the subject in Chapter 4.

If *you want specifics about employer-initiated schemes* on annualised hours, multi-skilling, outsourcing and the use of temporary employees you will find all this in Chapter 2, with advice on getting going in Chapter 4.

If you are interested in the technology-linked features of flexibility, these are fully covered in Chapter 3, including examples of implementing schemes.

If *you are looking for legal guidance*, you will find this in each specific chapter. For example, guidance on the Flexible Working Regulations 2002 is given in Chapter 1, while the complex legal status of temporary workers is discussed in Chapter 2. Please remember that new legislation is continually being introduced, and the courts, in both the UK and Europe, continue to make new interpretations of current law, so you should check out the current situation on one of the reference websites or with a legal authority before you take any irrevocable action.

If you are looking for a summary of how to start up and run a scheme, you will find this in Chapter 4, where it is discussed in general terms, such as initiating a policy or monitoring a scheme, and there is also specific summarised guidance in each area of flexibility.

If it is the process of selling the concept and ideas around the organisation that has caused you headaches, then please turn to Chapter 5 for guidance.

NOTE

1   Hot-desking is a practice for increasing flexibility where more than one employee can use a single workstation and desk space as required. It recognises that employee mobility often leaves desks unused, and tries to increase efficiency.

1

Working out the work–life balance: the employee demand for flexible working

INTRODUCTION

Flexible working has been around in some form ever since work was invented. Employees have always needed to be flexible to allow for those unpredictable circumstances that affect us from time to time, and good employers have recognised this and been able to adapt practices accordingly. However, there are now three distinct factors driving the need to recognise and encourage further flexibility:

- legislation
- unpredictability
- the nature of work.

First, legislation about the employee–employer relationship has created the need for a response. For example under the 2002 Flexible Working (Eligibility, Complaints and Remedies) Regulations, eligible employees who have been in 26 weeks' continuous employment have the right to request a contract variation to allow flexible working which will facilitate child care.

In total there have been around 50 pieces of UK legislation since the late 1970s that pertain to aspects of flexible working. The field has become increasingly more complicated, and the government has sought, perhaps paradoxically, to provide a regulatory background for practices that might previously have been subject to less formal agreement.

Second, employees experience levels of unpredictability in their work and non-work lives that have not generally been the norm previously, just as do the businesses they work for. Even for white-collar professionals, the well-ordered nine-to-five routine of life is far less common than in previous, less changeable eras. Employers that refuse to recruit from the pool of those who seek non-standard employment patterns are missing out on a whole raft of talent that their competitors will happily include.

Those seeking to retain and motivate higher-ability workers, or who want to become 'employers of choice', need to allow for this in their HR practices.

The final key driver is even more fundamental. It lies in the nature of work itself. For many people in developed economies the rise of 'knowledge work'[1] means this has significantly changed. Knowledge work creates jobs that depend less on physical and more on mental ability. Knowledge work is often far less reliant than physical work on time and physical location, so the opportunity or necessity has grown to work from remote locations, outside 'normal' office hours.

This chapter is about the likely impact and future challenges of these three drivers on the HR function.

THE (RE)QUEST FOR FLEXIBILITY

Figure 1 gives the procedural overview for a typical flexible working request. While there is no standard response to flexibility requests, the reasons behind the request will largely determine the appropriate response, which will need to combine the needs of the requester, legislative compliance, industry best practice, and the overall needs and objectives of the organisation.

All employers need to know the latest legal position. At the moment the law in brief says they must 'consider seriously' requests to work flexibly made by an employee who is parent with a child aged under 6, or a disabled child under 18. But as you will see from this book, it might be profitable to consider the applicability of flexible working to other groups also.

Qualification for flexible working

To make a request for flexible working under the statutory right employees must fulfil certain criteria. Employees must:

- be the mother, father, guardian or foster parent of the child in question, or the husband, wife or partner of one of these individuals

- have responsibility or expect to have responsibility for bringing up the child

- make the application as a means of enabling them to care for the child

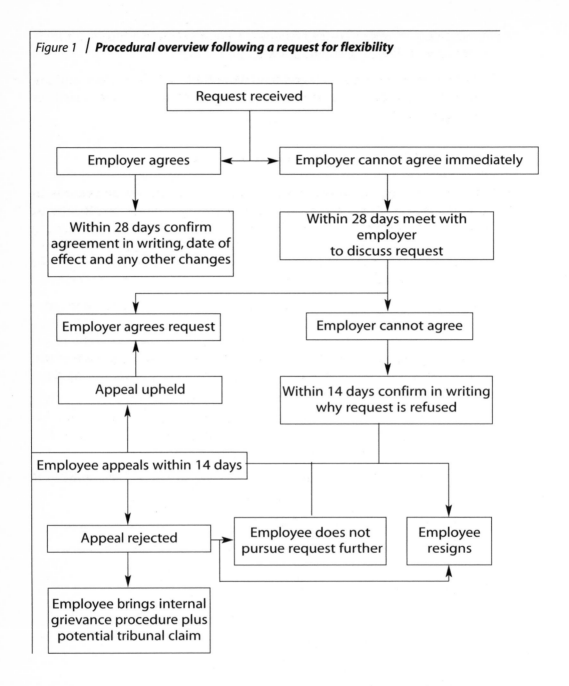

Figure 1 | ***Procedural overview following a request for flexibility***

- have worked for the employer continuously for at least 26 weeks before making the application

- have made no other application in the previous 12 months

- be willing to agree a change in their working pattern with a corresponding drop in pay if necessary (for example if they want to move from full to part-time work).

The child concerned must be aged under 6 or under 18 if disabled, and the application must be made at least two weeks before the child's sixth or eighteenth birthday.

Implementation of statutory flexible working

Under the law both parties are expected to follow correct procedures in implementing flexible working. These procedures require employees to prepare a detailed written application well in advance of when they want to change their working pattern. This application must include a clear plan of how the new pattern would work, and must show that the changes will not impact adversely on the organisation.

Once the application is received the employer has 28 days in which to meet with the employee, to decide a start date for the new arrangements if they are agreed, or consider alternatives. The employee has the right to be accompanied at the meeting. The companion must be an employee of the same organisation. If the application is agreed, the employer has 14 days to write to the employee confirming the new arrangements.

If the application is to be rejected, clear business reasons must be supplied why the proposed arrangements will not work in this case. The refusal must be dated, and allow for an appeals procedure.

Refusal to allow flexible working under this legislation is only allowed if there is a clear business reason. Examples of such reasons are:

- There will be a burden of extra costs.
- There will be a detrimental effect on the ability to meet customer demand.
- Work cannot be reorganised amongst other employees.
- Additional employees required cannot be recruited.
- There will be a detrimental effect on quality.
- There will be a detrimental effect on performance.
- There is insufficient work available when the employee proposes to work.
- There are planned structural changes.

Where an application to work flexibly has been refused, the employee has the right to appeal. If the employee wishes to appeal he or she must do so in writing within 14 days of the letter of refusal being sent. There must then be another meeting to hear the appeal within 14 days of receipt of the appeal letter. After the meeting the employer has another 14 days in which to confirm in writing whether the original refusal is to be confirmed or not.

If the appeal fails and the employee feels his or her request has not been considered seriously, he or she might consider taking further steps. Examples include the invocation of any formal company grievance procedure, or bringing in a third party to mediate.

If the employer has not followed the correct procedures, or the refusal decision was based on incorrect facts, the employee can make a formal complaint to an employment tribunal or to the ACAS arbitration scheme. If it can be shown that the employer has not followed correct procedures, the application will have to be reconsidered, and the employer may have to make compensatory payments to the requester. The amount of compensation is limited to a maximum of eight weeks' pay, and there is a limit to the weekly amount.

Typical groups who are likely to request access to flexible working are:

- labour market returners (such as the long-term sick or parents)
- carers
- older employees
- downshifters
- multiple career 'portfolio workers'.

Table 1 outlines typical scenarios for each category, covering legal rights, best practice, and the key issues that need to be considered.

BUSINESS BENEFITS AND RISKS FROM FLEXIBILITY

Table 1 offers a quick description of some flexible working options. The rest of this chapter offers more detailed considerations about the implications of each of the groups identified from the HR practitioner perspective.

Labour market returners

The legal rights of this group depend on both statutory considerations for those eligible and any contractual agreements in force at the time of their departure. Companies offering extended leave of absence will generally undertake to re-employ on the same conditions as when the employee left. This is becoming increasingly problematic, as the pace of change within organisations is such that someone who exits for only a year may find the place he or she returns to very different. Also if the reason for the departure is developmental (for example to study full-time for professional qualifications), returning employees will expect some recognition in status or employment conditions on their return.

The way that these and other groups of employees are managed from the HR perspective will be a significant factor in enhancing or detracting from the employer brand. As people look for more opportunities for career breaks or self-development opportunities, organisations that can assist with paid or unpaid sabbatical leave will have an edge in the recruitment market for key employees.

If the absence was taken for developmental purposes, best practice would include sharing in the development planning process and working out a resource plan which makes it clear how and where the returner would fit in on his or her return.

Where the absence has been for family, medical or health reasons, employers can enhance re-employability by maintaining the relationship with the individual, allowing contact to be continued and increased as the medical condition allows. Such situations will often result in gradual reintroductions, with the employee coming back to work on a part-time basis prior to resuming full duties.

Case study 1

Balancing work and family commitments through flexible working: Dawn Cooper

Dawn is in her early thirties, and she recently changed to working flexibly with the same employer (an independent recruitment consultancy) to fit in with her family arrangements. She has two children under 6, Lucy and Tom. She works flexibly around 15 hours per week, and sticks to the school timetable, meaning that she works 36 weeks per year. For her the main advantage of working flexibly is the opportunity it gives her to return to the workforce and continue her career. She is also able to continue working with clients that she has known and developed good relationships with over a number of years. This is obviously beneficial to her employer as well. Because of her willingness to work flexibly, Dawn thinks she

Table 1 / **Supporting the request for flexibility**

Requesting groups	Labour market returners	Carers	Older employees	Downshifters	Portfolio workers
Typical scenario	Returning to work after childbirth or period of full time study.	Job sharing to enable employee to look after the young or infirm.	Approaching retirement or looking to explore new opportunities.	Seeking to redress work/life balance issues or instigate career change.	Working for a series of multiple employers, often on a project basis.
Legal aspects to be considered in addition to those normally applicable e.g. equal pay regulations	Statutory maternity leave. Statutory adoption leave and pay. Statutory paternity leave and pay (including unpaid leave).	Time off for dependants (unpaid). The right to request flexible working.	European legislation has laid down that rules outlawing age discrimination must be in force by 2006.	Time off for dependants (unpaid).The right to request flexible working. Part time Workers Regulations 2000.	Contractual agreements. Data Protection Act 1998. Contracts (Rights of Third Parties) Act 1999. Fixed Term Employees Regulations, 2002.

Table 1 / Continued

Requesting groups	Labour market returners	Carers	Older employees	Downshifters	Portfolio workers
Best practice options available	Planned absence periods such as sabbaticals, or career breaks, where regular contact is maintained with the employee. Retainers may be paid on the understanding that the return to work will occur.	Planned sharing of role responsibilities to ensure consistency. Regular update meetings for job sharers, reviews of sharing arrangements to ensure compatibility with overall objectives.	Pre-retirement planning from individual and organisation perspective. Knowledge acquisition process to be completed prior to departure.	Mutually beneficial agreement around continued commitment. Planned 'handover' period to ensure consistency with new staff.	Project worker support mechanisms, 'Chinese walls' around sensitive information. Technological back up to ensure continuity of project with handovers.
Key issues for employers	Lack of currency of knowledge. Loss of status for returning employee. Disruption of departure/re-entry. Returner/employer circumstances changing.	Lack of flexibility around start/finish times due to outside commitments.	High level of knowledge and experience of the business needs to be captured.	Loss of key worker. Could be indicative of high stress levels being experienced.	Confidentiality issues. Unfavourable comparisons with 'conventional' employees.

achieves far more than she did before, particularly as many of her clients are also working flexibly. She is able to understand the issues they are dealing with and the needs they have from her first-hand experience.

> *I recognise that I am lucky with my current employer because we can be flexible in a fairly informal way. If I feel able to do more hours then I do and we just adjust my income at the end of the month to compensate. So long as I can validate what I have been doing, they are willing to negotiate and trust me because I have been with the company for some time*

Because Dawn works for a smaller outfit she finds that there is less restriction from rules and policies and procedures. This means she can often communicate her working time and needs to change it electronically. She is able to work from home if she needs to, as much of her work is on telephone and via e-mail.

> *I did previously work for a large national recruitment consultancy where they had a policy of not allowing part-time workers. This was based on their view that the roles required a full-time commitment.*

Dawn finds that working flexibly is a good way of obtaining the right work–life balance, and it gives her a positive perspective on both. She is able to combine her two roles very well because of the flexibility she enjoys. On the downside, because Dawn is the secondary income source for her family, she finds that finding time to deal with any sickness or problems with her children is usually down to her, not her partner Andy, who has a more traditional role as director of an estate agency.

> *Balancing my commitment to the workplace and the contribution I make with the commitment to my family can be a tough call at times, because you can get pulled in two directions.*

Another drawback Dawn had faced is the difficulty that part-time workers have over career advancement. It is not normal for part-time employees to have too much high-level control over their workloads or goals in terms of content, as they tend to be on the end of projects rather than managing them. Dawn misses the fact that she used to be in charge of a whole area and could allocate tasks to others when she was full-time. Also she highlighted that for the part-time or flexible worker, operating in a team environment can be stressful. When you are not there, team or project decisions still have to be made, and you often find yourself coming back to a situation where things have changed significantly and you do not always know the background reasons.

> *You have to accept that you have limitations in terms of your contribution when you are a part-timer. You obviously lose out on salary and other benefits that full-time people get. But when you go into the workplace I find that that you don't tend to contribute to the social side of things that much because you can't keep up with all of the gossip and things that people do alongside their work. There is much less social interaction and much more of a business focus.*

When asked if she would ever return to traditional, full-time, nine-to-five working, Dawn felt that it was probably unrealistic for her to consider doing so for two main reasons. Firstly she felt that she had taken on another 'job' as a mother and with her family responsibilities, but she also admitted that she really enjoyed the benefits of flexibility too much to seek a return to standard working. In her current work pattern she is often asked, and is able, to work outside normal hours at times that better suit her other life demands.

> *I think the more flexible you can be, the better it is from the employee's perspective, as you can tie in a whole range of non-work activities with getting your work done. You would never be able to do this in a traditional office environment.*

Dawn did report that sometimes relationships with full-time employees in the same organisation can be strained. She experienced problems when she was recently asked to manage the branch on a part-time basis, while still working flexibly. The idea was that she was able to increase her office hours to 20 per week and the other 20 of the normal 40-hour office week she was to be at home, but available via e-mail or phone to staff who had any problems. While the system worked all right when Dawn was in the office, she soon found that the staff were hostile to being 'managed' from a distance.

> *I felt that the business was not really getting the benefit from this way of working, and if people require to be monitored and managed, as they did, they really needed someone to be there full-time.*

Part-time employees, Dawn believes, are always under pressure to prove that they are contributing something, in comparison with full-time colleagues who are naturally able to achieve more.

Even though part-time employees tend to be more focused when they are at work as they know they have to do so much in a short time. Full-time employees often see the part-time people as having a privilege, but they don't often think about the down-sides of being part-time.

Dawn also reported that she is seeing a real rise in the number of people who are working flexibly and/or working from home at least for part of the week. She thought that the drive for change was coming from both sides of the employment relationship. Depending on how long they had been with the company and the experience they have, the company may be very happy to hang on to people even in a part-time capacity rather than lose them alto-gether. At the same time the employee who goes part-time gets some continuity of income and keeps in touch with the world of work.

Dawn offers the following advice to people thinking of following her example and working flexibly:

Start by listing out the advantages to both you and your employer of being flexible worker, and see if the benefits look like they are going to outweigh the likely problems. You also need to think carefully about what happens when your needs or the business needs change, as they so often do. Flexible working might be mutually beneficial for a short period, but you can never take anything for granted over the long term these days.

Some people in this category will be returning to the labour market after a complete break: that is, they have no previous relationship with their new employer. In these situations the emphasis is on HR to provide re-entry support for such recruits along the line of more commonly used induction processes, but tailored to the specific needs of older, more experienced groups.

Older returners are unlikely to need help in setting up accommodation or bank accounts, for example, but they might benefit from refresher training in customer service, or on understanding the technological side of their work role, which will inevitably have moved on since they were last employed.

One of the chief advantages to the employer of recruiting in this market is that the returners can become more effective staff members more quickly than raw recruits, so HR needs to take the responsibility for ensuring anything is done that can ease the process. More mature returners have been successful in the retail 'do it yourself' environment, where companies like B&Q and Homebase have deliberately used this labour pool to enhance both their flexibility and the quality of customer care.

HR issues in handling returners seeking to work flexibly

The traditional 'cradle to grave' employment pattern, where both sides of the employment relationship were happy to stay together from induction to retirement, is increasingly being challenged by people in this group.

- HR experts have to prepare policies and practices that will facilitate this change by enabling those who want to join, leave and rejoin the labour market to do so.

- As a minimum, ensure legal compliance for those eligible for extended absence via legislation.

- Where circumstances dictate that recruitment is more of a battle, and workers with key skills or experience prove to be difficult to hold on to, the HR response needs to be very different.

- Identification (via a knowledge audit) of high-risk areas where knowledge or experience is scarce would be an effective starting point. From here it is possible to plan for the future, incorporating the needs of those who wish to exit the organisation temporarily and those seeking to re-enter.

Employment contracts will need to be amended to take into account the new conditions. Employers might also seek to agree a trial period to ensure that the changes made are actually working out as expected. Employees' pay and holiday entitlement will need to be adjusted.

A further issue to consider is the disruption factor of employees left behind, who may need to cover for the absentee. HR policies on handover and business continuity need to be prepared to ensure that such an impact is minimised.

Carers

Legal considerations for this group include the right not to be treated unfairly in relation to full-time colleagues, the right to ask for flexible working, and the right to unpaid leave to take care of emergencies involving dependants without fear of dismissal or discrimination upon their return.

The position of an employee seeking to work flexibly to fulfil a caring role fits into one of two distinct categories. The first is where emergency care is needed, and it is only expected to be required for a few days. In this situation, good employers can be expected to take a 'reasonable' position. Indeed they would be liable for sanction if they refused to allow the employee to have unpaid time off. Depending on the role of the employee and the circumstances of the case, it might be justifiable for the employer to request that the employee ensures that any high-risk work commitments can be covered by colleagues. The second category is where the care is expected to be long-term and the employee therefore requests to work flexibly or reduced hours to cope.

This category will require a different response from the employer depending on the role of the employee, the value placed on that employee's contribution, and the likely ability to adequately replace his or her skill and experience. Offering flexible working where possible so that employees can work around their caring obligations will inevitably generate goodwill. Against this has to be weighed the drawback of part-time employees not being as available as their full-time counterparts.

HR issues in handling carers seeking to work flexibly

- Ensure that they are still able to play their full role in the organisation.

- Guard against exclusion deliberately or accidentally from activities and opportunities that their full-time colleagues experience.

- If the organisation has a large proportion of people in this category, it might be advisable to set up some sort of forum (virtual or real) where those benefiting from flexible working can communicate or discuss HR issues specific to them.

Once again contractual changes might be required to cover changes in hours, holidays and payment.

Older employees

There is no specific legislation in this field relating solely to 'older employees', but an increasing number of employees are looking to wind down from full-time work gradually rather than in one jump. They may actually see this as an opportunity to extend their working life beyond the normal retirement age.

From the employer side there are also opportunities to use flexible working to ease older, often more senior members of the organisation into retirement.

Flexibility around retirement can generally take two forms. First there is flexibility over the date of retirement, which might be used to extend or curtail employment. The other form is to vary the meaning of the word 'retirement' from being a final and total conclusion to being a more phased process, allowing retirees to become more accustomed to not working, and giving the organisation the opportunity to safely phase in younger employees.

Phasing retirement to allow for some downloading of expertise makes good business sense if the person about to leave has developed unique key knowledge and experience from which that others can benefit.

Knowledge acquisition projects have been carried out on soon to be retiring employees by Rolls Royce in the UK and HSBC around the world. In both cases the executives who participated in the projects found them to be both useful and satisfying ways of rounding off their careers.

HR issues in handling older employees seeking to work flexibly

From the HR perspective, older workers seeking to work flexibly present few really distinct problems, aside from the possibility that they might be in positions of seniority which could restrict opportunities for job-sharing. According to the CIPD Survey, Age, Pensions and Retirement (2003), 31 per cent of employees in their fifties want to work beyond their normal retirement age, and 8 per cent do not want to retire formally. Add to this the increasingly accepted view that moving from a highly stressed workplace to no work in one fell swoop is actually bad for one's health, and it makes sense for the HR function to be in a position to support flexible retirement schemes as and when they are requested by employees, or needed by the organisation.

Once again contractual changes will need to be introduced to reflect the new arrangements over issues such as hours, pay and holiday entitlement.

Downshifters

People can seek to downshift for a wide range of reasons. Some will not be seeking to work any fewer hours, but will be seeking less stressful work roles; others will simply be wanting to spend less time working. Still more may be looking to downshift in order that they can commit to more volunteer activity. From the HR perspective, monitoring requests for downshifting gives valuable information to help with the construction of appropriate responses.

Someone who sees downshifting as a stress avoidance remedy is possibly acting after the event, giving cause for concern over why the stress was allowed to build up. Negotiations in such a position will have to take account of the individual's worth to the organisation, even in a reduced capacity, versus the costs of offloading some of the workload to other employees or a new hire. Moving someone completely on to less stressful duties requires that such a position is available, and where it is available, a decision on what changes in compensation would be appropriate. The HR manager also needs to consider whether such a move is to be temporary or permanent. In either case, best practice requires clarity on both sides to avoid disputes and confusion at a later date.

The case of the downshifter who just wants to work restricted hours is one where standard HR processes will need to be revised. In an organisation where flexible working is not normally practised, this can be a challenge. Managers may be wary that agreement to allow one person to move to fewer hours will open the floodgates for potential chaos, with everyone working a different pattern. This does not have to be the case, and it will be the responsibility of the HR function to ensure that if downshifting is to be supported as a legitimate flexible working practice, it is done with a degree of order and logic.

Case study 2

Flexible working leads to downshifting: Geoff Joles

Geoff left a full-time position with a large international corporation in 2003. He had been employed as a management development special-ist for this organisation for over six years. Although he was too young to opt for complete retirement, a major restructure within the company left him with reduced options for doing the kind of work he wanted to do, so he decided to take the opportunity to leave relatively secure, perma-nent employment and go into flexible working on his own account.

Geoff now provides training and consultancy support to a whole range of organisations seeking to improve their effectiveness through better relationships or working practices.

> *Necessity was the mother of invention for me as I found myself unable to make the kind of contribution I wanted with my employer, so I decided to go back to what I was doing before I worked for them, when I was independent.*

Geoff sees the main advantage of flexible working in allowing him to do more interesting work than he ever could in his traditional, full-time role. Because he has a very good network of contacts in his field, he did not find it a problem to secure enough work, and was even able to turn down projects that he thought were not going to be very stimulating or exciting. Now when he finds a project that is really to his liking he can commit himself to it fully.

> *I have been really fortunate in being able to complete work for a rich mixture of organisations and different types of interventions they needed. Some were short-term, and others were longer-term but for me they have all met my chief criterion, which is about making an clear impact on the organisation.*

The downside of flexible working for Geoff is the uncertainty of not knowing if work bookings are going to come, although he has not found it a problem in his first year of operating in this mode. One of the ways that Geoff covers the problem of needing to be readily available at short notice but also keeping his existing projects ticking over is through his use of an informal network of colleagues and partners. He trusts them to share the workload when he is too thinly spread, and they reciprocate with him when he is available to do the things they cannot do.

> *I am not keen on the selling side of business development so I have a couple of contacts where they do specialise in generating new business or cold calling, for me to pitch into once they have the projects up and running, which suits me fine.*

When I asked Geoff if he was concerned about not having a full diary, he said the beauty of being a flexible worker is that your diary is as full as you want it to be, and he has to be careful to set boundaries around time he wants to reserve for time off and non-working activities.

He did recognise that getting the balance right between working and enjoying life as a flexible worker was a challenge that needed some time and thought. Geoff was unsure whether he would ever go back to full-time, traditional employment, as he said:

> *I have learned to never say never, as circumstances can change so quickly these days that if somebody offered me a traditional job I might consider it depending on the nature of the work. But the*

reality is I think that in my field the vast majority of work is so variable now that it cannot really be done in a nine-to-five scenario.

Even when I was a full-time employee, I always tried to work in a fairly flexible way, often doing things at odd hours and being available to my clients when they needed me. If this meant going out to dinner or making a breakfast meeting, then that is what I did. So I guess I was really operating very flexibly even in a very structured environment.

One of the criticisms that is often heard about flexible working, particularly in the field of consulting, is that customer relationships are often brief and quite transactionary. Geoff felt that this was no different really to the situation in many companies now, where movement and turnover of clients and staff is often such that people have to spend a lot of time on relationship maintenance issues.

Flexible workers have to be good at building relationships quickly and maintaining them often at a distance as they will not have the normal day-to-day client contact. The way that works best for me is to try to work mostly in an advisory role, where you can give people the space for reflection, and often be a neutral sounding board for their views and ideas which they cannot often get in their own organisations.

Geoff did not feel that he really missed anything too much from the days when he was a full-time employee, although he did recognise that the feeling of continuity that some people got from being employed was perhaps something he did not have any more. He quickly added:

The level of volatility that is experienced by many people in even big organisations now is such that the stability and certainty that used to be around has largely disappeared. I think that some people do refuse to admit it but the old days of having a stable 'job for life' are long gone.

Geoff uses his personal contact networks extensively as a compensation for the lack of regular contact he would experience in work. He often meets up with people, to share experiences and foster learning around what each of them is up to, and which techniques are working well. He places a high degree of importance on the building and maintaining of a personal support network for people working largely on their own like him, and recognises that this is probably something he needs to spend more time on than he does.

In advising people thinking about flexible working, Geoff thought that he was very fortunate in having established a financial buffer zone from previous employment, so that he knew he had the time to gradually ease into his new way of working. Where people did not have this advantage, he thought they needed to be clear about their transition to flexible working by spending time in exploring what they wanted to achieve from flexibility, and then being focused:

> *People I know who have not done well in the flexible working/consultancy sphere are those who were not really clear about what they wanted to do, and ended up having an unclear proposition to the market. You have to be able to explain what you are offering in clear language that the market you want to be in understands.*

Of course it would be easier for the organisation, particularly the HR area, if a 'one size fits all' approach could be sustained, and for some companies this may be possible, but the weight of demand for flexibility suggests that good HR practice is to prepare for the day when downshifting becomes more common alongside other forms of flexibility.

HR issues with downshifters seeking to work flexibly

- Downshifters are usually happy to work less time or on less demanding projects for a commensurate reduction in reward from the employer.

- What the downshifting employee wants is to be able to spend more time doing non-work activity, so offering the usual financial incentives will have less of an impact on this group.

- If the employer can offer flexible rewards that lead to better use of time, the downshifter will generally be more satisfied.

- Downshifting employees typically do not wish to engage in long-term career-enhancing activities like taking extra responsibility, or committing to longer-term development.

A further issue for organisations to consider is the view that having a large proportion of downshifting employees in this position may serve to place an extra burden on those employees who are working full-time.

Portfolio workers

This category of employee has rights under the 2000 Part-Time Workers Act, to not be given unfavourable treatment in relation to full-time workers, alongside other normal employment legislation. Again, those seeking to work in this manner will have a range of motivations. Some will be looking to find more interesting or different experiences, and may be tempted into full-time once the right opportunity comes along; others will see portfolio working as a part of bigger lifestyle choices, allowing them the time they need to pursue other interests.

Employers can derive a range of benefits from encouraging the use of portfolio workers. They bring outside experience to the organisation which can enhance performance, and they will also have a contact network that can be utilised to secure new business or add resources to existing programmes. Top-level portfolio workers will be in demand precisely because they have the leading-edge skills or experience that cannot be found through normal recruitment channels.

Case study 3

Portfolio working: Martyn Laycock, Managing Transitions

Martyn is a living example of what Charles Handy famously called a 'portfolio worker'. He is self-employed, with his own consultancy business called Managing Transitions, and works on a range of projects for different employers, after a career mainly in the financial services arena. This case study outlines the range of activities he undertakes.

Martyn is an independent management and training consultant specialising in marketing, change, knowledge and project management; he left mainstream banking in 1992 and has since developed his own successful business, built steadily and purposefully on personal relationships and personal service. He is in many ways typical of a generation of 'fifty-somethings', an enthusiastic player in Charles Handy's 'portfolio society', with a wide range of interests and activities, where, as he says, work and leisure seem to 'comfortably overlap'.

Martyn describes himself as a 'lifelong learner', having completed professional banking, finance and marketing qualifications between 1968 and 1990, undertaken an MBA through Henley Management College in the early 1990s, then recently signed on to do a knowledge-management focused DBA in Management and Leadership through University of Greenwich Business School. He learned the benefits of online communication and research as well as the rudiments of e-business at Henley, and has constantly over the last 10 or so years sought to use modern information and communication technology (ICT) to enhance both his business and personal life, helping him live up to the old adage, 'work smarter not harder'. He believes this works well for him.

He extends his business domains and coverage – not to mention his personal knowledge base and his income – through a number of networks, partnerships and collaborations, virtually all of which he manages electronically. He travels extensively, using his home office as his business base and depends upon 'always-on' broadband connectivity, business web-mail, and two things he says he is rarely without: a state-of-the-art Toshiba satellite laptop and an advanced Sony Ericsson global-roam PDA/mobile communications centre. These help him, he says, 'keep in touch wherever in the world I might be, working, travelling or even on vacation'.

When asked to take us through a typical working day, he found it hard to think what a 'typical' day would be, as the diversity of his lifestyle and the way he generates and does business almost precludes this. 'Some days I work long hours, others I "flex" things to incorporate leisure and social aspects.' The best he could do, was offer us the following example:

A day in the life of a portfolio worker

Monday 29 March

05:30 An 'early riser' and into his home office: three steps from the bedroom and just two from the bathroom. His office is a library crammed with business and management books, journals and research reports, and around £5,000 worth of equipment: the desktop PC, a laptop, printer/copier/scanner, two phones and a digital camcorder/camera and edit suite.

Martyn checks for any messages and texts as he opens up e-mails to review items that have come in during Sunday and overnight. (He worked part of Saturday, putting the finishing touches to a new one-day Leadership workshop, and also progressing a presentation for a conference to be held in April.)

There are e-mails from Australia (regarding a large conference he is co-organising in London in August) and from an 'organisational complexity' expert in Washington DC. There is also an opportunity to apply online for Funding from IBM, working on behalf of one of his clients. He has also received updated schedules and budgets from an Oxford-based business with which he is working to develop the programme for an exhibition, London Enterprise 2004, in October, and e-assignments from a couple of MBA students he works with from the university.

He also opens a couple of e-invoices from associates, and is reminded that he needs to issue his own e-invoices this week, to four different organisations. All are submitted electronically, and six of these will be paid electronically.

There is just time next to check the business bank account, and ensure that payments due in from last month are safely in, before **06:45**: he departs for the local gym where he has arranged an **09:00** meeting in the members' area with the London-based representative of the global media company.

By **10:15** he is back at his home base, reading a number of e-mails that have come in as a result of his own sent out early that morning. A major bank client in nearby Canary Wharf has requested a 45-minute postponement of a meeting that, it is now suggested, will also include a brief lunch. Martyn quickly e-mails agreement to this, which means he can now catch up electronically on some work he is doing for the London Knowledge Network (a collaboration of 14 large London-based organisations that are implementing knowledge management, run by the University of Greenwich). He updates the network website with a report from an event on Measuring Intangibles that he chaired last week. He downloads the latest *Knowledge Management Newsletter* from Ark Group, for whom he is co-authoring an article on change management, and then sends a draft communication to the network administrator to accompany a new events schedule he has finalised electronically with a colleague at the end of the previous week.

By **12:00** he is in Canary Wharf, discussing 'e' and 'blended' learning issues at a bank's headquarters. He is delighted that the client has installed 'wi-fi' connectivity as, along with showing a draft presentation, he is also quickly able to connect his laptop to the

Internet and review *in situ* with his client some learning-focused websites that instantly add value to their discussions.

By **13:30** business is concluded, and Martyn is on his way by train, collecting his voice mails, texts and e-mails as he travels to North London, where he will deliver the seventh module this month as part of a London Development Agency-funded business start-up course.

At **17:30** he leaves his business start-up people to progress their online business plan templates, and has time to catch up again on e- and voice mails before attending a Docklands Business Club meeting, where he rubs shoulders with 30 other business people, discussing how technology can positively assist businesses to become more efficient and more effective. The networking is great as usual, and he hands out several business cards and discusses one potentially good business proposition, before returning home at **21:00** feeling this has been another rewarding day.

Not all portfolio workers have to cram quite so much into one day, and Martyn finds that working flexibly suits his lifestyle, as well as being cost-effective and efficient. For him the main advantage of flexible working is that it allows him to meet with clients on their terms.

> *My clients and potential clients don't want to spend hours and hours talking to me, but by working flexibly and being mobile I can keep in touch with decision makers and move knowledge and information around confidentially with the objective of helping them to do business better.*

> *This way of working is cost-effective to both parties. Also I can have several contracts on the go at the same time, and flex between them, because I don't have to go to an office. I often have to train people in time management, and when I do, I emphasise that they must use their time between home and work productively, particularly as for some people the time involved has becoming a real brake on their productivity, if they spend three or four hours every day effectively doing nothing but commuting.*

Martyn has been able to set up his administrative arrangements to be quick and flexible, as all his invoicing and payments received are carried out electronically.

> *I do know some people who have tried it [working from home] and they just can't make it work. They get too easily distracted by other*

family members or things they have to do before they get to the work. If you have distractions but you still want to work flexibly from home, you just have to discipline yourself. Ideally if you can, set aside a room where everyone knows your work happens, and you cannot be disturbed when you are in there. This is easier for me because I happen to be an early riser, and I can do a lot of my stuff between 5:00 am and the time that everyone else is starting work at 9:00. I often send out e-mails very early in the day, go to the gym or do some other domestic stuff, and then get back online later to see how people have responded.

Martyn sees this need for self-discipline is the only real downside of flexible working, alongside the lack of personal contact, which he thinks some flexible workers might find difficult. He gets round this problem by making sure he gets to know as many people as he can whenever he works with a client. He makes a point of not just dealing with the project manager or sponsor, but also with his or her secretary or administrative team. This way he gets to feel more of a member of the operation, and can understand better the needs and requirements. He can also often tap in to the resources of the project sponsoring company more readily. Sometimes this really pays off, because he can then call on these people for support or guidance when the primary contact is not available.

A further downside is the reliance that Martyn and other flexible workers have on technology. If systems go offline for long periods this type of flexible worker's world stops. Where possible, a back-up is required. Martyn has established this again through contacts he has developed over the years, so he knows that he can always use a desk in a nearby office temporarily as a stop-gap.

On the upside, though, technology allows me to pitch for projects internationally, using materials and ideas from a range of sources without actually having to physically be in any one place.

As an example, Martyn told about a major project he was currently pitching for with associates for a company in Tokyo, even though he had never been to Japan.

When asked if he thought he would ever go back to traditional nine-to-five working, he said:

No way, absolutely not. It would just frustrate the hell out of me because it is just not efficient. I would spend more time on tubes and transportation than I want to, and then there is this thing called 'office politics', which I think means that you end up spending more time doing non-productive things than you do on the really productive income-generating activity.

Keeping the relationships alive is a key skill for flexible working, and Martyn has every sort of communications technology at his disposal to ensure that whenever anyone needs to contact him, they can.

Wherever I am in the world I have 'tri-band' telephone, web-based e-mail and a 'wi-fi' state of the art laptop. So provided I can get to any sort of connectivity I can be found, if I want to be found.

Martyn was employed in banking for 28 years, and then spent five years full-time in a university. From these periods of full-time working he does not miss much in his move to flexibility. He was also able to benefit from his experience of an early move towards flexible working, where he observed one of his employers impose a new flexible working scheme on people who did not really want to work flexibly. The objective of the move was purely to remove costs by enabling sales people and their managers in an asset finance function to work from home. They were all given allowances to cover the use of their homes, but it all went wrong because the company did not think about the issues that really face home workers. Problems with low morale, intrusive distractions, self-motiviation and moving from the 'going to the office' culture were just not properly considered. These problems were made all the more serious because this was an imposed change, not a consultative one. Alongside the problems that the home workers had, the few employees who were left to provide support from an office environment felt that they were being asked to do more work, while the flexible workers were unsupervised and, in their eyes, doing much less work.

Martyn was able to make the move to flexibility relatively free of fear, as he deliberately transitioned gradually from full-time to flexible, over a period of time. He feels he learned the craft of flexible working slowly and became more confident as a result. He can now talk to clients and prospects on their terms and in their premises. He also joined a number of unofficial support groups, so that when he has any problems that the traditional employee would naturally refer to other colleagues, he has a ready-made sounding board and source of personal support.

Martyn offers the following advice for people thinking about moving into flexible working.

> *If you are working for a corporate, think very carefully about how much your life is affected by the company you work for, the relationships, the activities and support systems. While it is easy to be critical of many organisations, it might be that you are actually more dependent on them than you think. If you are going to go flexible, make sure you have the right kit, you know how to use it, and an area to work in where you know you won't be disturbed.*

On the downside, portfolio workers bring some key HR issues such as the need for non-standard contracts. Disputes can occur if both parties are not clear about the length and continuity of employment offered. Payment of portfolio workers can also be a financial problem, as some will prefer to be paid on a consultancy fee basis, rather than through standard PAYE methods.

As with other instances of flexible working, decisions may need to be made about how non-standard compensation benefits such as share options and SAYE schemes are to be applied to those working in less than a full-time capacity.

There is also a possible issue of split loyalty to different employers. The portfolio worker will typically have a range of projects at once, and will seek to convince each employer that he or she is performing well in each one. There is always the option of insisting on non-competitive working, although this condition would be hard to police and enforce. But we should not get carried away with the idea that this is something new and unique, as a number of members of the building and construction trades have successfully used the concept of multiple project working for many years.

HR issues in handling a portfolio workforce

- True portfolio workers are motivated by the interest and excitement that their projects generate.

- To attract and retain the best people requires not only selection and creation of good quality projects, but also giving the portfolio worker appropriate roles within them.

- Portfolio workers will not work on only one project in one organisation at a time.

In addition the typical portfolio worker may have a range of projects on the go, which any one employing organisation knows nothing about. It is largely the responsibility of the individual workers to manage this for themselves, but the consequences of burn-out and issues of conflicting confidentiality suggest that a key role for HR is in keeping at least an informal eye on the work–life balance of the organisation's portfolio workers.

Contractual problems might arise for this group, as employers often stipulate that for reasons of confidentiality, working for competitor organisations is not permitted. Definitions of competitor need to be carefully worded now that many organisations have diversified into a range of products and areas.

TYPES OF FLEXIBILITY

The examples already covered demonstrate the wide range of options available. All of them will be covered in more detail in the following chapter. Here some of the main options are introduced.

Part-time work

If the normal definition of full-time work involves employees working 35 to 45 hours in a standard working week, then anyone working less than this can be classified as part-time. As an option, this sort of working offers flexibility to both sides, as the employer can organise part-time employees to meet peaks of work demand and release them when they are not required. Employees get the freedom to spend their time as they please outside of the contracted hours. Variations of the number of hours worked can be negotiated almost on a daily basis for even more flexibility.

Such variability rests on cooperation and goodwill from both sides, so it is essential that the HR function strives to ensure that the employment relationship remains amicable. Employers who demand that their part-time workers constantly do more hours than they want to do are not recognising the needs of the group. Equally, part-time employees who are never able to offer flexibility around working time are less valuable than those who can.

The main strain on the HR function of such a working pattern falls into the 'HR transactions' area. Systems and procedures for monitoring things such as working time, productivity, leave and absence, all feeding through into reward calculations, will need to be implemented in such a way that they can flex easily to meet the needs for part-time working. Time spent on automation at the implementation stage, in ensuring that HR transactions are technologically slick and control data is easily gathered, will be rewarded as the introduction of part-time working commences. The last thing the HR manager needs is to be forever chasing basic data, and line managers will not thank them for passing over the responsibility.

Career breaks

Taking an extended break from employment for a whole range of reasons has now become more popular, as more opportunities exist for people to study, travel or try alternative ways to earn a living. For example, in the past only a small percentage of students would indulge in a 'gap year' between school and university, or between university years. Now it has become much more the norm to take such a break. Some universities have had a long tradition of offering staff sabbatical breaks from their normal work.

Businesses need to assess their responses to such a demand as it inevitably increases. They can also look to assess the value that a potential employee who has taken a long break from traditional working might bring, in terms of a diversity of experience. Where companies are in need of creativity and innovation, people who by their experience have been exposed to different cultures, ideas and practices might be a valuable asset. HR managers who are involved in the recruitment of such applicants will need to explore how the experience gained outside work will be beneficial to the organisation, rather than dismiss it as a 'gap on the CV'.

Career breaks are also an excellent way of being able to retain staff the organisation values when they leave for child care reasons or because of other family commitments. Formal arrangements over the length of the break, any continuation of contact, and what the employee is entitled to on his or her return, will need to be devised. HR managers will need to specify what the position will be over service-related benefits such as pension and leave entitlements. If the employee is on a career break, is he or she maintaining his/her 'employed status', or does it constitute a break of service?

Flexible hours

An extension of more traditional part-time working is the move towards flexible hours. There are various models in practice, such as annual hours contracts, where the employee completes a total number of hours over the year, before any overtime payment is triggered. This sort of scheme gives flexibility again to meet variations in workload, and is particularly useful in seasonal occupations.

At the more traditional end of the spectrum, many companies have implemented flexible working through flexitime for many years. These systems give flexibility to employees to deal with one-off or occasional commitments requiring release from work, and give a way of recognising where employees need to work longer hours for specific problems.

All flexitime agreements have a daily common core period during which employees are expected to be present, typically from 10:00 to 16:00. Flexibility is then allowed typically between 07:00 and 19:00, whereby employees can work earlier or later than the norm as required. By 'clocking up' extra hours the employee can typically build up to bank full or part days to be taken as additional leave.

Working from home

Using appropriate technology, it has now become relatively easy for many employees to spend at least part of their time working from home. This element of flexible working has advantages for the employee such as:

- eliminating commuting time and costs
- fitting in work with household commitments such as being present for a delivery
- allowing focus on specific tasks away from the distractions of the office.

On the downside, employees who work from home may have problems if they miss out on key events while they are away from their normal workplace. There may also be difficulties in finding an appropriate place to work in the home environment, which after all is not usually designed with work uses in mind.

It is often good practice to conduct a risk assessment prior to commencement of the home-working activity. This can be carried out by the employee. Typical areas to be considered include:

- Seating and layout of the employee's computer workstation.
- Electrical equipment: is it tested and certified safe?
- Extension leads for telephones, PCs and printers must be safe.
- Lighting, heating and ventilation must all be adequate.

Case study 4: The loneliness of the long-distance flexible home worker

Kathy Whymark works as a corporate development manager for a leading university educational provider in the UK. Her job involves the provision of distance learning and development, so not only is she herself a remote worker, but she is dealing day to day with the issues of those studying at a distance. She has been a home-based worker for over three years, and when interviewed she provided excellent first-hand examples of how the experience of being a home-based worker has both good and bad features.

Kathy has a sales and marketing role, and a geographic territory that covers the south-east of the country. She believes it makes sense for her to be home based as she does most of her productive work out in the field, talking to clients and prospective customers. If she was based in an office she would obviously waste time travelling to and from it.

She sees the main advantages of working flexibly from the employee's point of view as being able to organise many aspects of your work and non-work life much more easily, because flexible working means really having the potential to do seven-day, 24-hour working. If some non-work priority or issue needs to be dealt with, it is up to her to rearrange her day to cater for it, and she can compensate by working later in the evening or at the weekend.

In addition Kathy sees working flexibly from home as far more efficient in terms of managing time, because distractions can be minimised. If she is working on a particular problem or issue she can devote full attention to it until it is finished, and she does not have to break off, like colleagues who are office-based, to deal with other calls on her time.

Working flexibly in this example gives the employee a high level of control over what distractions are allowed, as technological support is on hand to deal with telephone and e-mail contacts which can be stored for later in the work day.

The downsides of flexible working as Kathy sees them mainly involve lack of contact with other employees, resulting in her being somewhat 'forgotten' by her office-based team, and the loss of connection with others in her organisation. She also sees a real danger in flexible home workers succumbing to overworking. As there is no real control over when you start and finish work, you can find yourself working far longer than you intended, particularly if the work is interesting or stimulating. Kathy's home office is always available and open, so there is a temptation for people to become 'workaholics' at the expense of their other activities.

Kathy emphasised the drawbacks of not having regular contact with other people, and offered some examples of her strategies for dealing with this. For example she makes extra effort to arrange meetings around lunchtimes with colleagues so that she can combine business discussions with time to catch up on the non-work information that many of her office-based counterparts take for granted.

When asked if she thought she could ever return to a traditional fixed nine-to-five working arrangement, her reply was decisive and clear. She felt that she would never wish to return to traditional working patterns after experiencing the benefits and freedom of flexibility.

> *I would find it very difficult to go back to being in an office from nine to five and to be closely managed now. I am used to being very self-reliant and sorting myself out if I have any problems. I really enjoy the variety that I get in my job, as I am out and about more than I am at my home office. So to sit in one office all the time would be very difficult for me now.*

When it comes to her relationship with customers, Kathy has some ongoing contacts that last, but the majority are one-off contacts, where building rapport and developing understanding is quite difficult. For this reason Kathy thinks that the sort of flexible working she does, where ongoing customer contact is quite limited, requires a special set of skills.

Her relationship with colleagues is restricted, as with all flexible workers, as contact can often be quite minimal. She does not meet all the members of her team from week to week. Again she has made a deliberate effort to contact some of her team by telephone regularly to keep in touch. Kathy feels that people who do not work flexibly sometimes underestimate the demands placed on flexible workers, and tend to see only the freedom of flexibility and none of the downsides:

> *Some of my colleagues are probably jealous of the freedom I have to work flexibly. They might think that when I am not visiting clients I am not working. But what they do not realise is that there is a lot of administration, chasing, report writing and things that need to be done when you are not on the road. All these tasks need to be self-managed and you have to be able to make yourself do the chores or it will soon get out of control. A lot is*

down to trust, and to be an effective flexible worker you have to win trust. It is not just about being able to have a doctor's appointment without asking for permission.

What Kathy really misses about not working in a traditional manner is the ongoing connectivity with other people. She believes that the technology that can ensure electronic connections is no real substitute for eyeball-to-eyeball relationships. She has also found that her 40-mile separation from her workbase means that when she does meet with her colleagues, it tends to be far more formal, as many of the usual barriers that exist between people do not get the chance to be broken down in the normal way.

From the employer side, Kathy believes that it is essential that employers ensure that the technological support for remote or flexible workers is 'state of the art'. Connectivity is everything for the flexible worker, and if computer systems are unreliable or regularly go offline for updates, the consequences of this for the flexible employee need to be taken into account. There is also, she feels, a responsibility on the employer to communicate more proactively with remote workers who do not have access to internal memos, noticeboards or the general office grapevine to find out what is going on.

Teambuilding and social events also need to ensure flexible workers are included. If this is not done well, the organisation will lose out, as the remote workers will not be considered for inclusion in new projects or new initiatives where they can really add value.

Flexible or home-based workers really have to work hard at building and maintaining their profile, particularly if they want to be considered for promotion opportunities. There is a tendency to be forgotten about because you just are not present as often as other people.

If anyone asked Kathy for advice if they were considering moving into a flexible working position, she would say:

It's a great way to work but do make sure you are fully supported by your employer. Make sure if you can that the organisation you are moving into is going to recognise your skills and talents as a flexible worker. I meet many people who say they could not work the way I do because you do need to have the self-discipline that other more traditional roles don't really require.

Working remotely (teleworking)

Extending the concept of flexible working to its limit suggests that some work can be truly location-independent. That is, it does not have to be done in one specific location. Working remotely, or 'teleworking', is the term given to someone who is able to work in this way. Wherever the job role does not require direct contact with equipment or the personal touch with customers, there is potential to employ this form of flexibility.

In the early 1990s many commentators predicted that teleworking would grow to become the new norm for many organisations. Some of these predictions were augmented by the sponsorship of interested parties such as telecommunications companies, who naturally enough sought to encourage companies to move in this direction. As yet the revolution is largely still awaited, but the arrival in some areas of broadband telecommunications may well make the case for teleworking more compelling.

Remote working still requires infrastructure support, and there has been a growth of suppliers willing to provide temporary or itinerant 'serviced offices' where employees of a range of companies can work and take advantage of shared facilities.

Job-sharing

According to an IDS study from September 2000, the incidence of job-sharing in the UK has doubled in the past decade, with over 200,000 people participating. Where the phenomenon might have been regarded as predominantly a public sector one in the past, it is now increasingly becoming adopted more generally, as private sector organisations recognise the gains that can be made from the practice. Informal arrangements are also making way for more regulated schemes, which often have at their heart a desire to improve the work–life balance of the participants.

Most job-sharers are female, and have dependent children. For them the benefits are clear, but there are also advantages claimed by employers who favour job-sharing:

- increased staff retention
- higher motivation
- improved effectiveness through pooling of experience
- reduced absenteeism
- greater continuity through holidays and sickness.

On the downside the potential disadvantages of job-sharing include:

- resistance from line managers
- finding the right match (skills and complementary hours/days) of job-share partners
- increased costs of training or equipment provided
- communication issues between the sharers.

One potential minefield for HR managers seeking to monitor or introduce job-sharing arrangements involves clearly defining benefits and rewards for the sharers. On the surface a 50:50 split between the sharers does not seem too difficult to achieve, but the devil is in the detail. For example if two people share a job where one does Monday to Wednesday and the other does Thursday to Saturday, what do you do about statutory bank holidays, which predominantly fall on a Monday? This will obviously favour the employee who works the first part of the week unless an arrangement is put in place.

Existing employees who move to job-shares will generally sign a new contract detailing their change of status and outlining that benefits, including sick pay, pensions, maternity pay, profit sharing and share options, are pro rata to those of a full-time employee. As job-sharing becomes more common-place in more senior positions, other issues around benefits that cannot be divided, such as provision of a company car, will also need to be resolved.

There is no legal right to job-share, although care must be taken to ensure that employers act within reason and do not fall foul of indirect discrimination in insisting that employees work full-time. The case of *Robinson v Oddbins Limited* (4224/95) demonstrates the issues involved. In this case a branch manager for the wine merchant sought to reduce and fix her working hours after she returned to work following maternity leave. The industrial tribunal heard that contractually she had to work 39 hours, plus any additional hours necessary (typically 50 hours per week). The company claimed that in the role of a branch manager flexibility was essential, and job-sharing would not be possible. The tribunal was not satisfied with the reasons put forward by Oddbins, and particular criticism was levelled by the tribunals at the employer's failure to consider the option to job-share 'properly or with an open mind'.

CONCLUSION

This chapter has introduced some of the major considerations for those seeking to support flexible working, by taking some particular examples and looking at the cases of four real flexible workers. Of course not all flexible working possibilities are covered, but the main principles here will still apply. The message for HR managers from this chapter should be quite clear: the flexible working revolution is already here, and it is offering challenges, risks and opportunities. Through reading the rest of this book, thinking the issues through, and the preparation of an effective HR response incorporating the concerns and features we have covered, the ability to grasp the challenge, avoid the risks and maximise any opportunities will be easier to achieve.

NOTE

1   A knowledge worker is anyone who routinely makes a decision (based on his or her knowledge) about what he/she must do during the working day. That is, he or she is not reliant on 'the job' or other factors to dictate the pattern of work.

2

Making the business case: the employer push for flexible working

Back in 1994, the Institute of Personnel and Development (now CIPD) produced a landmark position paper called 'People make the difference' (IPD 1994). It made use of much futurologists' prognosis of economies and organisations in the twenty-first century, identifying the driving forces for change and indicating the ways organisations need to respond in the way they manage their employees.

The paper identified four main drivers:

- customers demanding products and services increasingly customised to their needs, with satisfaction standards increasingly established by global competition
- reductions in international trade barriers leading to new overseas competitors, especially in Pacific Rim countries, in mature production and service sectors
- profound technological developments affecting the way we work, do business and communicate
- public sector financial restraints, political pressures for higher value for money and privatisation, and market testing, all heavily audited.

In response to these drivers, the IPD recommended a much more effective use of human assets, and much of this was directed towards implementing flexible working or changes that supported flexible working. On the list were:

- commitment to personal training and development with a view to increasing employee adaptability
- development of a flexible workforce, capable of carrying out a variety of tasks and projects

- decentralisation of decision-making so that self-managed, trained and adaptable teams could control and take responsibility for their own output and service provision.

Other areas of recommendations had a very clear link to flexibility. Customer orientation to meet the needs of both internal and external customers cannot take place without organising systems of employment that cover 24 hours, seven days a week for many retail and service organisations, and this implies a considerable use of part-time labour, outsourcing and annualised hours. Total Quality and lean organisation initiatives, quicker response times and continuous improvements need a multi-skilled workforce, and one that has a commitment to the organisation's goals and philosophy.

The theme of this chapter is that many successful organisations have taken on board these challenges and searched for more efficient ways of using those expensive and unique costs, their employees' time and productivity. Their aims are to meet the organisation's specific needs, and they are all different. That is why the concept of 'best practice' is rarely employed in the context of flexibility. Annualised hours may be vital for a seasonal manufacturer but of little significance for a government agency. Part-time employees are the hub of many catering and hospitality organisations, but not a key feature of a power station. Outsourcing is a huge success in one sector but struggles to be viable in another sector.

This chapter sets out the main flexible systems that employers have initiated: in the fields of temporal flexibility, the use of annualised hours; in occupational flexibility, the use of multi-skilling; and in numerical flexibility, the use of outsourcing and temporary employment. You will find a number of cases and explanations of the challenges involved.

ANNUALISED HOURS

Introduction

A few years ago, Frigoscandia, based in Norfolk, was faced by a growing problem, quite literally. Its 700 employees were finding it increasingly difficult to process, freeze and pack up to 75,000 tons of fresh vegetables and chips within the limited harvest period, and yet provide an efficient storage and distribution service to large supermarkets and other customers for the remainder of the year.

The answer was not simply to take on large numbers of temporary employees in the summer months. Although flexible, this labour needed training and considerable supervision. It was not always possible to pinpoint precisely the harvest dates or the size of the harvest from one year to another. A sizeable core of skilled employees needed to be retained throughout the year to process imported rice and vegetables and to service customers' requirements. The crux was that the hours in the summer would always be considerably in excess of those in the remaining months. The problem was that employees were on a contract of 37.5 hours per week, summer or winter. They were willing to work extra hours, with individual weeks of 84 hours not uncommon; but these hours would be on overtime at premium rates. Come October, there was not the work to keep all the workforce fully occupied for 37.5 hours. Then the company heard about annualised hours.

Within three months, its methods of operation had altered fundamentally. Labour costs had reduced and scheduling was operated far more efficiently. More surprisingly, employees were more committed and morale was far higher. Shareholders received higher profits and customers a more professional and reliable service. It was clear that there was something rather unusual about a system that appeared to benefit all stakeholders in the business.

Background to annualised hours

The Scandinavians are credited with the first formal large-scale introduction of an annual hours scheme in 1977, when the Swedish paperboard industry produced an innovative system to cover 24-hour, seven-day working at its paper mills. The chemicals industry and other continuous process industries moved tentatively into this unknown territory, often through extensive national union negotiations.

Schemes began to appear in the UK in the early 1980s, but were slow at first to develop. An ACAS survey in 1988 found 3 per cent of employees working under a formal scheme but this had risen to 4.3 per cent by 2002, equivalent to a 820,000 full-time employees, according to the Labour Force Survey (Labour Market Trends 2002). Part of the slow development in this area can be accounted for by the overall decline in the manufacturing sector, where more than 5 per cent of staff work on annualised hours.

The context for annualised hours

Schemes have traditionally been associated with a manufacturing context. The majority of schemes still take place either where seasonal operations occur, such as in cheese processing (Express Foods) or television manufacturing (Matsushita), or where production is required around the clock, seven days a week (Continental Can). In these types of situations, detailed rostering is required, usually some weeks or months ahead, to ensure that labour is evenly distributed to meet the foreseen requirements. A key objective in all the schemes is to reduce or totally eliminate the level of overtime. The Working Time Directive has often been the trigger to take action over long working hours, especially with the likely eventual abandonment of the UK opt-out special arrangement.

It is now clear, however, that annualised hours are beginning to spread to more unusual domains, particularly in the service sector. The RAC converted its patrol staff to annualised hours in 1999, while the National Exhibition Centre (NEC) in Birmingham has implemented a variety of annualised hours schemes since the late 1990s. Royal and Sun (More Than division) operates schemes for sales and customer service claims handlers in call centres, allowing it to meet service demands more effectively. Schemes have spread to the hospitality sector (including Gleneagles Hotel – see Case study 5), where 24-hour service is required.

Case study 5: Annualised hours at Gleneagles Hotel

Gleneagles is one of the world's leading five-star hotels, with a world-wide reputation for fine dining, quality accommodation and superb sporting facilities. These facilities have little value unless they are accompanied by excellent service, and the hotel is constantly striving to improve here. In the mid-1990s, it became apparent that the system of relying on large numbers of casual staff and a degree of unpaid infor-mal overtime to meet the peak demands resulted in service quality which was not as consistently high as the management team wanted. The full-time staff turnover rate was also getting worse as the Scottish economy picked up.

Once management had looked at all the options available to meet the objectives, it was decided to use the knowledge base to establish reli-able forecasts of the labour supply demand throughout the year, down to a week-by-week and even hour-by-hour analysis, and then set up a working time change programme to meet this demand.

The hotel employed a senior partner from Working Time Solutions to carry out a thorough analysis, using briefings and interviews with staff at all levels. He investigated what was required and what types of system the staff would prefer to use to meet the demand. An interesting by-product of the process was to generate full awareness of the needs, and increase the feeling of involvement. One of the key

---

findings was that staff felt the system of being leaned on to work unpaid overtime was inequitable.

By using a complex business modelling process with sophisticated software tools, forecasts of throughput were translated into labour requirement models, and schedules which took into account staff preferences. From this, it was possible to draw up annual contracts with rostered hours for the year ahead, which included banked hours. Rosters are confirmed two to three weeks ahead, and all hours worked are recorded, leaving the team leaders and staff with precise knowledge of the cumulative hours to date. Subsequent shifts during the year can be balanced out appropriately. Some departments are highly seasonal, with large numbers of hours worked in season.

The new scheme began in 1998 with pilots in the food and beverage departments, and after the inevitable teething problems, the system has bedded in very well. By 2000 the improvements were clear, with staff turnover much reduced and the peak periods successfully covered with much fewer staff. Schemes have been gradually introduced in all the hotel's operations, with staff taking much of the initiative in planning and operating the systems. The sense of fairness in operating staffing levels and systems has greatly increased, with much greater transparency and an elimination of staff being asked to work unpaid overtime. The policy has developed to have staff working overall slightly over their hours target, with a small balancing payment made at the year end.

Bernard Murphy is hotel manager with responsibility for introducing the scheme. His advice is:

> *Do make sure to keep a firm hand on the scheme or it will drift. And ensure that staff are fully informed and involved in what happens – without their involvement, it is highly unlikely it will work smoothly.*

Source: Working Time Solutions.

Manchester Airport's scheme began in 1992, and covers around 200 engineering supervisors, technicians and operatives. Yorkshire TV and ITN News have both operated schemes since the late 1980s covering a combined total of 1,000 employees. A large number of local authorities, including Surrey, Kent and Hertfordshire County Councils and South Oxfordshire, Wrekin and Strathkelvin District Councils, have responded to the efficiency needs of government edicts on best value and meeting local consumers' needs by introducing a variety of schemes. Some cover seasonal services such as leisure centres and grounds maintenance, and others have a comprehensive approach, with annualised hours as part of a comprehensive flexibility system tied in with increasing home working and work–life balance measures.

A number of schemes have started in the transport sector. The European Passenger Service started the Channel Tunnel operation with annual hours contracts for its operating staff, while London, Tilbury and Southend Rail, a train-operating company, moved to a similar arrangement in the mid-1990s. In the logistics sector, 80 per cent of Tesco's distribution workforce is covered, including junior managers, clerical staff and drivers. while another example is Excel Logistics.

Such schemes are rarely introduced as a stand-alone initiative. In the majority of cases, it is part of a wider integrative process of change, incorporating a raft of HRM initiatives. For example, at Unilever's Bestfoods Purfleet site, annualised hours formed part of the 'New Look Employment' contract, with increased flexibility, harmonisation of terms and conditions, and an integrated salary structure. HP Foods introduced its scheme in 2000 at Birmingham and Worcester alongside a general restructuring which included a change in shift patterns, substantial automation, a move to teamworking and revisions to the pay structure.

Similarly, at Bristol and West Building Society, annualised hours was included within the package called 'Towards 2000' aimed at harmonising conditions for employees working in three different sectors of the organisation: estate agencies, the building society, and financial advice. Welsh Water introduced a 1991 'Partnership Agreement' which, alongside annual hours, gave single status, single-table negotiating and a unified pay structure.

How a scheme works

The essential feature of a scheme is, as the name suggests, a replacement of a weekly hours contract by one covering the whole year. Instead of a 38-hour week, for example, an employee will be on a contract of 1,976 hours for the year. The pay system is also changed so that the employee receives a fixed monthly payment, no matter how many shifts are worked that month. How much the pay system changes is discussed later. That is the easy part.

Alongside this change is an evaluation of the basic labour requirement for all the operations involved. This is not based on the existing staffing levels. It involves a careful analysis of the labour required if the operation runs completely smoothly, with no absenteeism, no machine breakdowns, no supply or quality problems, no industrial relations problems and no serious accidents. In the majority of cases, this evaluation takes place with the help of consultants, although in establishments where there is a high level of trust, the operational managers will carry out the analysis themselves. This is such a crucial activity and so central to the success of the entire scheme that the estimates have to be right. The usual British system of sorting out problems through overtime is not a solution under annual hours because the aim is to eliminate all overtime. Any absenteeism, or disruption of any sort that affects the work scheduling, has to be remedied by the system of reserve hours.

The annual hours are divided into sections, as shown in Table 2.

Rostered hours

If the labour requirements for the year are reasonably foreseeable, such as on an oil rig or the chemical industry on long-term supplier contracts, then an employee's hours will be rostered for the year. In this example, the 150 shifts could be worked on the basis of alternate weeks with six shifts on one week and none the next. A more complex shift pattern would spread the hours over days and nights. A key feature is that the amount of leisure time is extended by compressing the working time into a shorter period.

If the labour requirements are less predictable, such as in seasonal operations, they will be allocated on a basis of a general indication, such as 42 hours in summer and 30 hours in winter. (Redditch Council operates a scheme similar to this, worked out with the Unison union.) Hours are then scheduled one or two months ahead in detail, as the business requirements are clarified. For South Oxfordshire District Council, some staff can be rostered into nine-day fortnights and others can work higher hours in term-time and fewer hours in school holidays. Rostering can be achieved by using a specific software package, marketing by consultants in the area, or it can be delegated to the staff themselves, as in the NatWest Bank scheme, where the staff work out the best arrangements for all parties, within clear criteria and cost restraints (Holroyd 1999).

Table 2 | **Calculating annual hours**

Contracted annual hours total		*1,976*
Rostered hours, 150 shifts at 10 hours	*1,500*	
Holidays	*228*	*1,728*
Reserve hours:		*248*
Training hours	*60*	
Hours on call	*188*	*248*

Holidays

These are normally expressed as a number of hours, not of days, and are fixed under the standard rules that apply in the establishments. In most production environments the holidays are rostered into the shift system, but more flexibility can be allowed for them to be changed by mutual agreement. For example, NEC staff are able to swap shifts (Wustemann 1999b), as are most staff working under annualised hours in NHS trusts.

Reserve hours

It is reserve hours that define the scheme. (One commentator has called this 'the sexy part'.) Reserve hours are to be used when necessary for a number of reasons. First, they can be used for training. We have seen that team-working and multi-skilling are often an integral part of the changes implemented simultaneously with annual hours, so some of the reserve hours are used to train employees in alternative tasks on their shift, which qualifies them to become more flexible. There may be training in new systems introduced to aid efficiency and improve quality. Time may be spent in gaining a better understanding of associated functions such as dealing with suppliers or the distribution system. All this training is to enable the employee to respond quicker and more cooperatively to any problems that arise.

Second, they can be used to cover for absenteeism or for any difficulty faced on the shift. Employees will be rostered to be on call in case they are required. In these circumstances, they will have to be available so that they can be at the work site within an hour or so. They do not get paid anything extra for attending work on these occasions, as this is all included in the monthly wage.

The number of reserve hours varies greatly across schemes. At Scottish Power, it varies between 100 and 150 hours, depending on occupational group. For Royal and Sun, it can be as high as 240 hours, coming down to 204 hours for Manchester Airport technical and support staff. At Irish Fertiliser, 58 of the reserve hours are rostered for training, safety meetings and special tasks, such as plant overhauls.

If the scheme works well, a situation will emerge where those reserve hours are not all used. This is certainly the clear intention of the British Nuclear Fuels scheme, where 100 hours are banked. The number of times employees need to be called in should drop as disruptions caused by absenteeism, machine breakdowns and materials supply problems fall. That is the main objective of the scheme, and one that defines the most successful schemes.

Inducements to employees

Employees are usually sceptical when new working practices are proposed. For those who work considerable overtime, annual hours is bad news. When complex rosters with 24-hour working are announced, this presents problems for employees with a regular weekly social commitment. For supervisors and managers who rule through the carrot of overtime, there has to be a fundamental change in their outlook on good management practice.

For many employees, however, there are some immediate benefits. They get a guaranteed income each month, which assists in obtaining mortgages and other credit. Their rosters are set out in advance, and they know when they are on call and when they are completely at leisure. They tend to welcome the change to the scheme without any further inducement.

Both these groups tend to be minorities, though, and it is the bulk of employees in the middle, who work some overtime and have some commitments, who need to be convinced. The views of any trade unions have to be considered. Overtime has always been a thorn in the side of trade unions. Although many of their members enjoy the opportunity to work overtime, and press for union help in negotiating improved overtime conditions, unions see overtime as a barrier to employment. They can see a group of their members out of work and trying to exist on social security at the same time as they see other members working excessive hours and earning high wages.

The introduction of annual hours therefore presents no problems of principle for trade unions – quite the contrary, it is welcomed by many with considerable enthusiasm as reflecting good union practice. All that are left to negotiate are the terms and conditions. As these are specific to the work site, to the rostering system and to the methods of working, the union is not often faced with problems over national or local practices or parity with other local firms. The dangers associated with trend-setting agreements are therefore much reduced. Unions and management, with only terms and conditions to agree, rarely have too much trouble in coming to an amiable agreement.

The agreements usually have at least two parts. There is some *reduction in the weekly hours* with no loss of earnings. It may be quite small, for example from 38 to 37.5 hours, or it may be bolder, stretching the reduction over three years from 38 to as low as 36. When Peugeot Motor Company introduced its scheme in 1997, it reduced the working year by 20 hours and also added an additional day of holiday.

Since the late 1980s, employers have fought very hard against any reduction in the working week, as an hour off the week is equivalent to a pay increase of almost 3 per cent. At a time of low inflation, this is a huge concession. They have also been aware that there is no great support for reducing hours in itself from employees, unless it gives them the opportunity to work more hours at overtime rates. Introducing annual hours, however, gives employers the opportunity to meet union aspirations and get valuable proven concessions in return. Taking an hour off the week to make it 37 hours would mean a revision to the original calculation.

The rostered hours and holidays do not change, it is simply the reserve hours figure that reduces. As the aim is to try to avoid working reserve hours in any case, that may not be crucial to the organisation. In fact, it may be a concession that costs nothing.

The second element may be a *one-off inducement to accept the scheme*. This may be an across-the-board payment of say £250, or it may be related to the amount of actual overtime earnings by individual employees over the previous period, say two years. How it is paid depends a great deal on the number of high overtime earners, their importance to the organisation and their influence amongst their peers. If they are few in number and have little influence, the payment is likely to be across the board to generate general agreement to the scheme. If they are influential or a sizeable proportion of employees, then they are likely to get a more sympathetic ear, and the payments may be more variable.

There may be other items in the agreement. The way holidays are rostered and how they can be traded may become much more flexible. Decisions on leave for dentist appointments, seeing solicitors and the like may be delegated to local managers, rather than being based on a detailed, centrally determined policy. There may also be an offer of voluntary redundancy. Agreements often include a time-related guarantee of no compulsory redundancies through implementing the scheme.

Another option is to make further concessions dependent upon the success of the scheme, leaving a year or so for it to bed in and prove its cost-effectiveness.

Key benefits of the scheme

Saving in labour costs

Overtime operation is extremely costly. For ITN, the overtime bill prior to the introduction of annual hours was a crippling 21 per cent of staff costs, and this is not unusual. But there is a more subtle hidden cost. For the average operator, the temptation of overtime is difficult to resist. Overtime is usually paid at time and a half (double time on Sundays), so employees can add a sizeable chunk to their wages at the expense of a few hours of extra work.

Studies have found that overtime is habit-forming, and the employees' expenditure patterns can start to match the expectation that overtime will be regular. A reasonably high level of sickness and absenteeism from colleagues will give regular attenders overtime opportunities. They will be sympathetic to the difficulties of their absent colleagues. The machine breakdown or critical supplies running out is unfortunate for the company schedules but fortuitous to the operators. It is not far to the next step, which is for operators to assist in creating the overtime. Going just a little bit slower, and more rejections of poor quality work, for example, can lead to a need for overtime. Add on a little bit of absenteeism, and this will provide overtime for workmates as a quid pro quo.

Furthermore, it is not unusual for supervisors to be paid overtime in a traditional work set-up, and to covertly support this general approach, thereby guaranteeing overtime payments for themselves. Line managers may treat overtime as a 'comfort blanket' which allows them to match staffing to changing production targets or unexpected customer service demands. All this operates against the interest of the employer, and increases organisational costs.

Annual hours put a stop to all this. The elimination of overtime costs creates a substantial saving, and more than makes up for the increase in basic pay and any other inducements offered to gain acceptance to the scheme. Another saving is in the reduction in the workforce numbers that can be associated with the scheme. The average overall labour cost saving under annual hours is estimated at around half the overtime costs. In the case of ITN, this was as high as 10 per cent of overall labour costs.

Savings in labour costs leading to increased productivity have shown clearly in a number of schemes. For the RAC, productivity levels have risen by 8 per cent (IDS 2002), while the improved revenue stream at NEC has allowed the centre to take on ticketing contracts for events outside Birmingham, such as the Southampton Boat Show.

Improving commitment

Because overtime is eliminated completely, at least in the most ambitious and successful schemes, it does not take long for employees to realise that their way to gain under the scheme is to protect their reserve hours. If they are not called in for those reserve hours, they will have gained the equivalent of up to an extra five weeks' holiday. To ensure that they are not called in, they need to make sure that they are not required in the workplace. They need the elimination of absenteeism and sickness, of machine breakdowns and poor material supply. They need production schedules to be met on time. To achieve these goals, they need to work closely with their team-mates to ensure that any problems on the shift are overcome. Self-development by gaining new skills is vital, so that they can step into the place of an absent colleague rather than call in a replacement.

This change of attitude means that the objectives of the employers and the employees are aligned. They both want high production levels, and good-quality, on-time delivery.

Reducing absenteeism

Absenteeism reduces for two reasons. First, the increased sense of commitment leads to employees taking time off only when they are truly ill. Second, there is peer pressure to conform to high levels of attendance. When an employee is absent, it may be necessary for a colleague to be called in under the reserve hour scheme, and the absent employee will not be the most popular person in this circumstance! There have been a number of examples of a team demanding that management take action against a colleague with a poor attendance record.

In practice, the results can be surprisingly good. The absence level at NEC dropped from close to 15 per cent down to less than 8 per cent a year after the scheme was introduced. Other schemes have reported improvements of between 4 and 12 per cent.

Improved health and safety

It cannot be good for the long-term health of employees to work 55 or 60 hours a week, even if they have signed up to the opt-out on the Working Time Agreement, nor can it lead to efficient working. There is also an increased emphasis on employees taking regular leisure and relaxation time. More-over, there is anecdotal evidence of the number of accidents reducing under annual hours. This can be simply because employees have their eye on the ball, and because they know that an accident in the workplace can lead to employees being called in to help solve the inevitable production problems that result.

Improved teamworking and co-operation

Also associated with the increased employee commitment, there is evidence that employees work together better as a team and use their empowerment effectively. This may show itself in covering for an absent colleague, in arranging swaps on rotas or on holidays, or in implementing more ideas that improve the work systems. This has been a key feature of the Queens Hospital scheme (see Case study 6, on page oo). Teams are often given responsibility to organise their own breaks, to liaise on materials supply with purchasing departments, and to carry out basic maintenance on their machinery rather than wait for a specialist maintenance mechanic.

Difficulties encountered

There are always teething troubles whenever new schemes are introduced, and annual hours is no exception. The working hours and rosters can be complex and may need fine-tuning. For employees with children, the call-outs to use their reserve hours can create problems for childcare, which may be awkward or even impossible to arrange at short notice. This has been a particular problem at ITN News, and there have had to be special rostering and payment arrangements made in these cases.

There can be minor difficulties associated with employees starting and leaving during the course of an annual hours year, especially one that operates seasonally. The issue of paying back hours in these cases is a thorny one. The same applies in the case of an employee taking maternity leave during a slack period and coming back to work higher hours for the rest of the year. Introducing changes in shift patterns part-way through a year can also present difficulties.

Calling on reserve hours can sometimes be tricky. Organisations use different systems, including rotas and strict ordering, and agreements for employees to have up to three refusals a year for personal reasons. Employees can also be allowed to swap their reserve shift. At Boots Manufacturing's Strepsils packing facility, volunteers are initially sought before management turns to employees with the most reserve hours (IDS 2004a). All these arrangements are dependent on having employees with the required skills.

Having said this, there are surprisingly few reported major problems with the scheme operation. Moreover, very few schemes are started and then abandoned, and these usually occur due to a shift in the market place.

Variations in schemes

Very few schemes are identical, and new variations appear on a regular basis in the following areas.

Choice of contract hours

In a number of schemes, employees can choose their total annual hours and be paid accordingly. For example, at RAC Motoring Services, staff can sign up to reserve hours of zero, 92, 184, 276 or 368 (Warner 2000). Customer advisers at Alliance and Leicester have a choice of 787 or 936 hours per years as part-time employees, with working patterns agreed one month in advance. Saturdays and Sundays can be included in the work patterns (Suff 1998).

Other examples of employees having a choice of hours are also in the service sector. ITN offers three levels above and below the standard hours, and Bristol and West offers four part-time options.

Quarterly reserve hours

Rather than having a year-long bank of reserve hours, some companies have shorter periods. For example, Elida Gibbs aerosol factory divides the year into four quarters, and any reserve hours unused at the end of the quarter are written off. A similar arrangement operates at Lever Bros over a four-month period.

Case study 6: Annual hours at Queens Hospital

Opened in the early 1990s, Queens Hospital is a private acute hospital built in the grounds of a large NHS hospital. It has 33 beds and 140 permanent staff, with two multi-speciality wards treating both day-case and longer-stay patients, and a consulting room suite operating six days a week from 8:00 to 21:00.

For the first few years of operation, nursing staff worked an informal flexible rostering system. The rosters were issued two to four weeks ahead, and requests for changes in the rosters for personal or domestic reasons were dealt with sympathetically by department heads. In those circumstances, when roster swops could not be arranged, 'bank' nurses would be brought in.

In 1996 a further development took place. Queens Hospital is part of a larger health care group, and a system of annual hours had been gradually pioneered at a number of units within the group with considerable success. After full consultation with the staff, the system was introduced for those staff that wished to transfer onto the new arrangement immediately, and for all new recruits.

How it works

Staff are contracted onto full-time hours at 1,950 per annum or at various levels of part-time hours – 936 is a popular level. For each month they are issued with a provisional rota, and each employee indicates any areas of difficulty, or any extra time when he or she would be available and willing to work. The department head then looks at revisions that may be necessary, swaps that can easily be made, and efficient extra staffing based on indicated willingness to work. During that month, the workload may suddenly increase (say bad weather produces more orthopaedic work) and staff who had indicated availability may be asked to work. Sometimes the workload may drop as a result of, say, cancelled operations, and when this happens, the staff on the shift are asked if they would prefer not to work that day.

The year runs from January to December, and a running total of the hours worked is kept for each employee. Nobody exceeds his or her contracted annual hours total. Employees may choose to make themselves available for extra work from January to March, then work fewer hours in the summer months, or take an extra week of holiday. It may happen in the course of the year that one or two employees regularly work in excess of their provisional shift hours, and if it looks as if they could exceed the annual hours total, they could be paid overtime for those excess hours instead and have those hours deducted from the annual hours. This arrangement is not that common, however.

Anne Jones has been nursing director at Queens Hospital since it opened, and has seen the scheme develop:

> *The key to the scheme is the recognition that Queens Hospital is everybody's hospital – everybody needs to work with and for each other to make sure that it is successful. Without that genuine belief, the flexibility would become one-sided. Either the hospital would make excess demands on the staff to work shifts and rotas against their will, or the staff would exploit the system just for their own benefit. Neither of these is happening.*

One of the other key points is the need to have a multi-skilled nursing force, eager to perform extended roles in, say, venepuncture or ECG recordings because it is essential that the skills mix on the shifts is correct. Without these skills (and Queens Hospital strongly supports professional development for each employee) the flexibility would be more limited in practice.

Achievements of the scheme

For Queens Hospital, the staffing levels are always on line to meet the needs of the hospital's workload. With traditional shift patterns, if the workload is reduced for any reason, the nursing staff on that shift are under-utilised and resources are wasted. Overstaffing can be very costly. When a situation of reduced workload occurs under annual hours, the roster is reduced accordingly. The staff than work shifts when they are fully needed.

From the employees' viewpoint, it gives them a degree of flexibility to fit in their shifts with their domestic and private commitments within an environment that consciously tries to accommodate their needs.

Finally, Anne feels that:

> *It helps being quite a small unit so everybody knows each other. Often they will help out with each other's childcare needs, for example. Certainly they can see that the scheme is operated fairly to all concerned, which can be difficult in much larger NHS hospitals where rumours can circulate about unfair practices. The department heads, who also work under the scheme, find it successful and it presents them with few problems. Certainly, the principles of the scheme can easily be transferred to any NHS setting as long as the will to make it work is there.*

(For reasons of confidentiality, the name 'Queens Hospital' has been used in this case study. It is not the real name.)

Postscript

For Frigoscandia, the scheme has been a considerable success since its introduction in the early 1990s. It has not remained unchanged, however, and the company has not been wholly successful at eliminating all overtime. The culprits here are the major supermarkets, such as Tesco and Safeway. Frigoscandia can deal with the vagaries of harvesting and storage through its flexible rostering system, which is accepted and understood by the employees. What have proved more difficult to deal with are the ever-tightening demands of supermarkets for retrieval and delivery of their frozen products. What used to be a two-day order has now become a 10-hour order, as the supplies kept in the supermarkets have been cut to the bone. Come a couple of hot days, and the customer will require within hours large quantities of specified ice-cream, and other frozen goods pallets which are sure to be in the most awkward part of the massive storage depot. The reserve hours system finds difficulty coping with this, and a small amount of overtime is creeping back. It should be possible to give some forecast of the supermarket's demands, and to adjust the storage and labour requirements accordingly. Frigoscandia is working on this.

MULTI-SKILLING

Introduction

We have seen earlier in the book how the competitive context of the globalised economy has meant that organisations have had to examine every opportunity to improve performance and service while reducing costs. This has meant a huge concentration on increasing productivity and reducing the unit cost of employees.

By a unique twist of history, the development of the UK union structure left a post-war legacy of inter-union struggles, first between craft unions and unskilled unions, and second between the craft unions themselves to hold on to their members and the defined jobs. This led to a dire period of industrial relations in the 1960s and 1970s, where employers struggled to implement much-needed improvements in flexibility against intransigent unions determined to avoid any change that took jobs or members away from them.

By the 1980s, with a combination of anti-union legislation, union amalgamations, high unemployment and a lack of public sympathy for strikes and union self-indulgence, the employers' battle to win the right to reform and initiate substantial changes in working practices had been won. In manufacturing, this led to a wave of multi-skilling initiatives which has had a degree of success in the UK preserving some part of an industrial sector, even if it was much reduced. 3M (see Case study 7) is a case in point here.

In the service sector, which has been much less affected by union philosophies, multi-skilled workforces have been a fairly traditional concept, but the last 20 years have seen a concentration on refining the job focus, embedding certain key flexibility behaviours, and ensuring that employees have every opportunity of developing themselves, to improve the quality of the service and obtain higher customer satisfaction. This has

Case study 7: Multi-skilling at 3M Manufacturing

The 3M Aycliffe plant in County Durham employs 400 staff manufacturing around 100 million face respirators a year. In the face of stiff competition in the 1990s, the plant entered into a series of initiatives to increase productivity, improve quality and save costs, under the name Total Productive Manufacturing (TPM).

Each section (cell) has been involved in establishing its own milestones within the company's wider objectives. Targets are set in a wide number of areas, including output, down-time, quality levels, waste, asset-care and attendance, and the cell teams work out together how best to achieve these targets. One of the principal means is to achieve multi-skilling in tasks, and extensive training programmes have been set up and operated for some years. In one cell of 10 employees, complete interchangeability of jobs has been achieved, and cell members rotate jobs every four hours, while regular job exchange is very common within cells.

Each cell has responsibility for routine machine maintenance, and cell members have been taught these processes by maintenance staff, who have been freed up to deal with more challenging engineering problems. The barrier between production and engineering is being moved incrementally, arising from local need, rather than dictated central policy. Production employees want to avoid the frustration of waiting for maintenance, and have pushed to enhance their knowledge.

Supporting this process is a training schedule encouraging all production staff to achieve NVQ level 2 for operative and NVQ level 3 for team leaders, and the proportion of staff with this qualification has risen to nearly 50 per cent. There is extensive communication of training achievements through notice boards in each cell listing individuals' skill development and progress towards a qualification, and regular reports in the house magazine.

There is no immediate financial reward involved in the multi-skilling activities. Intrinsic rewards are the main driving force – increased confidence (many staff thought the qualification was beyond them), increased job knowledge, a relief from boredom, pride in their quality and housekeeping achievements have all been quoted in the regular feedback achieved in the plant. However, knowledge of a number of jobs does provide a greater opportunity for overtime, when it is available.

> Achievements of multi-skilling contribute towards an employee recognition and gainsharing scheme, where financial gains by the plant are shared with employees and teams based on their cell achievements.
>
> Source: author's research.

required employees to be familiar with a range of products or services, rather than just one, so any customer queries can be answered and the administrative processes completed quicker. These features are shown in the Nottingham City Hospital Trust case study (page 62).

Types of multi-skilling

There are two main types of multi-skilling, lateral and vertical.

Lateral multi-skilling is where an employee is trained in jobs at the same level: for example, learning all the jobs on an assembly line or learning sets of jobs on the same grade at the head office of a large bank.

Vertical multi-skilling is where an employee carries out jobs that are at a higher or lower level to his or her normal job. For example, on the assembly line, employees might carry out the cleaning and tidying of their work area and the receipt of incoming goods. These jobs would normally be ranked (and paid) at a lower level. Employees might also, as part of an empowered work team, take part in decisions on work schedules, shift patterns and holiday rotas which would previously have been carried out by a supervisor or manager.

It is not uncommon for both systems to be in place at the same time, as part of a general blurring of job roles and an encouragement towards efficient team functioning. A quarter of employer respondents to the UK Workplace Employee Relations survey in 1998 (Cully et al 1999) stated that there was a lot more task flexibility than five years earlier.

Does it work? There have been a number of academic studies associated with this initiative, nearly all of them very positive. For example, Murray and Gerhart (1998) studied two comparable US companies, one of which had multi-skilling and the other did not. At the end of three years, they found that the company with multi-skilling had 58 per cent greater productivity, 16 per cent lower labour costs and 82 per cent greater scrap reduction.

In reality, it is now an essential factor of all manufacturing. Without the drive for substantial, if not complete, interchangeability, companies would not survive against competitors with much cheaper labour in the globalised economy.

Benefits for organisations

Having a multi-skilled workforce can lead to huge benefits for the organisation:

- More effective deployment: employees can be utilised where they are required, moving from one job to another to plug gaps and help out. Waiting time is much reduced and the flow of work improved. For example, employees who are able to service their own machinery and deal with simple breakdowns save time in having to call out maintenance crews.

- Costs are cut because of the need for fewer staff specialising in only one function. Vertical multi-skilling can provide the opportunity for de-layering which, in turn, saves managerial, supervisory and unskilled costs.

- Multi-skilled employees have a much greater connection with their colleagues, understanding their needs and requirements. On the production line, for example, they are much less likely to pass on work that is not properly completed because they are personally aware of the problems this can cause. Similarly, in an office or call centre, a multi-skilled employee will not pass paperwork or customers on to the next stage in an operation unless it is done correctly, knowing the difficulties that incomplete paperwork can cause.

- Cover for sickness, holidays and other forms of absence is much easier to organise.

- Customer service should be much improved, with a multi-skilled employee knowing all the answers, rather than passing the customer from one person to another.

- As part of a high-commitment initiative, multi-skilling can provide much greater opportunities for increased employee involvement in the processes and practices, leading in turn to higher motivation and commitment.

- There is usually a much greater degree of co-operation in the change process, especially where the need for quick response to customer requirements is recognised.

Benefits for individuals

From an individual's viewpoint, the following benefits can be forthcoming:

- Having wider training can lead to greater employability both within the organisation and outside it.

- With job enlargement, the work usually becomes more interesting and challenging, with less chance of boredom creeping in. Having a greater understanding of more processes can widen the viewpoint and stimulate the interest.

- It can lead to a growth in personal confidence and self-worth, especially if the initiative is the first time anyone has suggested that an individual employee could become qualified for anything.

- There can be greater opportunity for employees to provide ideas for improvement and to be recognised by the organisation for their greater contribution. Their potential for eventual promotion is more likely to be recognised.

- There is less likelihood of being laid off and more opportunity of being redeployed when the employee's work is temporarily reduced.

- Higher pay is often associated with the initiative.

As with most forms of flexibility, effective multi-skilling can help to develop a positive psychological contract, with employees willing to change their ways of working by learning more tasks, while the organisation pays to make them more skilled and employable. This can be seen in case study 8, of a Nottingham hospital.

Case study 8: Multi-skilling clinical skills at Nottingham City Hospital

Having an operation cancelled is one of life's most unpleasant surprises, and hospitals will go to any length to try to avoid it. In 1999, Nottingham City Hospital NHS Trust devised a totally new system of operating to avoid the heavy cancellations caused by having the wrong set of skills available for its planned operations. By doing so, it not only performed far more efficiently but it also won the Nye Bevan award from the Department of Health.

The major problem was the separation of qualifications for the nurses who assisted anaesthetists and the nurses who assisted surgeons, who are known as operating department practitioners (ODPs). They worked within a different management hierarchy and had different terms and conditions, including varying shift rota systems. They certainly could not do each other's job. This meant that the right number of staff might be available for an operating session, but not the right mix of skills.

To solve the problem, the Trust had to make some fundamental changes, moving away from the Whitley Council straitjacket of pay and conditions. It did this through an extended process of consultation with staff to find a joint system of rotas and overtime that met the Trust's needs and had the greatest support from staff. When this was achieved, a new post was set up which combined the ODP positions with standard nursing roles.

New sets of competencies were defined for the new position, developed by the staff themselves, and training opportunities were created to allow staff to fill the skill gaps they did not possess. Previously, staff reached the top of their grade through annual increments, irrespective of skills or performance. Under the new system, staff had to gather evidence of their skills and produce a portfolio so they could meet the criteria for grade progress.

One of the interesting outcomes from the change has been the change of approach to learning. Previously, staff often indicated that they did not want to do something that was not part of their role; under the new system, staff often want to grasp an opportunity to gain experience so they can progress on their pay scale.

The outcome was exceptional, with a large reduction in the waiting list, far fewer cancellations and a cut in sickness absence from 7 to 5 per cent. There has also been a discernible improvement in co-operation between staff as they understand each other's roles much better.

Source: Johnson (1999).

Eliminating the cycle of failure

One of the greatest claims for success of multi-skilling is in breaking the cycle of failure, as set out in research by Schlesinger and Heskett (1992). Their research into low-pay service industries showed that organisations enter this cycle by tolerating high staff turnover, high absence and employee dissatisfaction. They pay low wages, simplify the job to sets of repetitive boring tasks which require little training, and see little point in investing in staff when they are likely to leave quickly. This response merely exacerbates the problem, with even higher degrees of dissatisfaction and high turnover. Moreover, the cycle produces poor attitudes and service from staff, while customers have a poor perception of the service.

To break the cycle, the research showed that employers had made a commitment to up-front expenditure of money and effort to achieve a vital, but largely invisible, competitive advantage. They spent less than their competitors on recruitment and basic training, but attracted the most performance-minded managers and front-line personnel. Their provision of a more satisfying work environment for effective performers often encouraged applicants whose personal philosophies fitted those of the employer, where customer satisfaction was paramount.

Discussion of major issues

Payment for multi-skilling

It is common, but not essential, for some form of payments to be associated with the achievement of multi-skilling (Homan 2000). The payment serves to motivate employees at all levels to support the scheme, and emphasises its importance to the organisation. However, there are some circumstances where payments may not be considered appropriate:

- In administrative and managerial areas where learning and carrying out a variety of jobs is considered quite normal.

- In manufacturing areas where moving to multi-skilling is one of the essential improvements that can help the organisation to survive in the face of a crisis.

It is also possible, as in the 3M case study, that intrinsic rewards will be sufficient for most employees to go along with the process.

Where payment is deemed essential, it can take the following forms:

- *Up-front payment to achieve agreement*: in Nottingham City Hospital, the restructuring of grades produced a higher basic pay grade for staff taking part in the scheme. This system is quite common where schemes are negotiated with trade unions and agreement is reached either with the help of a one-off payment or by increasing the basic pay for all concerned before the multi-skilling training starts.

- *Pay supplements*: in a banking case, supplements to the basic rate were paid at three levels of achievements with the total supplements adding up to around £2,000 per annum. Several manufacturing companies, including SKF and Peugeot, have operated a similar system.

- *Movement up the pay scale*: an alternative, less formal approach is for the multi-skilling achieved to be taken into account when salaries are reviewed and for employees to move up the salary scale within their grade or band over and above the annual increase.

Pay supplements or allowances need also to be considered for supervisors and managers. If these groups are involved in the hands-on training, they will need instructor training themselves. The successful achievement of multi-skilling within their department should certainly be part of their personal objectives. Their enthusiasm and leadership makes all the difference to success or failure.

Skill rewards are not necessarily in monetary terms. A scheme within Welcome Break motorway catering, called Staff Winners Award, recognised the achievements of staff under the various modules through badges and certificates.

How will trainees be chosen?

Some interesting research on employees who take successfully to multi-skilling came from a recent report on Dutch railways (Van de Velde and Van de Velde 2003). The important characteristics they found were:

- need for personal growth
- tendency for innovation
- general self-belief.

Although they found that these characteristics were more often found in younger and better-educated staff, all staff responded better when more freedom and autonomy were allowed and more personal support was given.

Once the detailed plan is drawn up, the number of employees and their skill requirements can be established. Personal development plans can then be drawn up for each employee. A decision has to be made whether the multi-skilling is to be voluntary or compulsory. It would make logical sense for this to be an inherent part of the contract, but for ease of changeover from existing contracts, it is often approached as a voluntary matter in the first place, as in Nottingham City Hospital Trust. Under most initiatives, where required it is compulsory for all new staff.

However, there have been some experiences where the number of employees willing to be trained is in excess of the number required in the plan. There is no point, of course, in gaining skills that will not be required.

SKF faced this problem at an early stage in its initiative, partly because of the perceived generosity of its payments for multi-skilling. After some early difficulties over accusations of favouritism, a deal was struck with the union to overcome the problem. Every three months a programme of multi-skilling requirements was put forward by management, detailing skills in each area and inviting applications from the relevant employees. Once the applications were in, a small mixed group representing line managers, supervisors and employees met, and if the applications exceeded the numbers required, discussions took place on who was chosen. A person's attendance service and current skills were considered, but in the early stages the choice was often made by lot. Overall, this was considered a much fairer system.

What methods of training will be used and will accreditation apply?

The options on training methods will very much depend on the environment. In small-scale operations, there is often no alternative to 'sitting by Nellie', with few formalities. For larger-scale operations, the learning process can be planned and monitored by trainers who then put the trainees through an agreed assessment method. This will range from a simple observation to the assessment of a learning log demonstrating the skills achieved.

Accreditation is usually achieved by entering a competence-based NVQ system, where skill sets are identified at specific NVQ levels, and employees work their way towards completing their set and achieving an NVQ, usually starting at level 1 and progressing to levels 2 and 3. These can follow an industry sector standard, or less frequently are tailor-made for an organisation. BHS (formerly British Home Stores) started down the NVQ route in the early 1990s but then switched to its own training and development package called 'Spotlight on Success'. All of the company's 14,000 employees were enrolled on the scheme, which consisted of 18 components (or acts). Employees completed the acts in two stages, with a monetary reward following success at each level.

Around the same time, Rhone-Poulenc Agriculture introduced an NVQ-based multi-skills progression system for its technicians to be completed over a three-year period.

NVQs can be seen as a transferable qualification, but the process is sometimes regarded as bureaucratic and additional accreditation costs are involved.

Developments in technology can make the learning and assessment process more formal. Barclaycall, for example, devised a computer-based learning system for modules of its training, supported by occasional tutoring and testing on the job.

Some dangers to avoid

Skills not being used

It is not always easy to forecast accurately the skills that will be required, and it is all too easy to over-estimate the expected volume, only to find that many employees have skills they do not use. This can be very expensive and have a bad effect on morale. It is imperative that the human resource plan detailing the required skills is constantly updated and evaluated, and that the bulk of the training takes place in small batches.

Underestimating the costs involved

When undertaking the programme, organisations must be aware of all the costs involved in training, loss of production, overtime to replace colleagues under training, assessment, training the trainers and accreditation, if applicable. Multi-skilling initiatives are not cheap, although they generally reap huge benefits in return.

Disruption of teams

The training and assessment must take place under a carefully planned programme to avoid disruption of key business activities and the reduction in team performance levels. Team members must appreciate the benefits from the outcomes to be willing to put up with the inevitable changes that occur in day-to-day activities.

Fear of exit of multi-skilled employees

There have always been concerns from employers that the high investment made in training staff will be lost when the trained staff walk out of the door to a competitor. Of course it does happen, but research evidence mostly concludes that increased training furthers the sense of loyalty to the organisation and leads to greater commitment. Certainly the Van de Velde study and may others have found this to be the case. Perhaps this fear is not well founded.

A final danger to avoid is explained by Stephen Taylor (2002), who describes the early part of his management training in a large hotel where he and fellow trainees were multi-skilled in all the basic hospitality activities. Unfortunately, they learnt them so quickly and were so competent that they became indispensable to the hotel management in plugging each and every daily labour gap, with the effect that there were severe delays until they moved on to their next stage of proper management training!

OUTSOURCING

Introduction

A young consultant from a reputable company was once giving an enthusiastic and earnest talk to the board of a medium-sized engineering company about the enormous benefits to be achieved by the new concept of 'outsourcing'. Companies all over the Midlands were taking up this innovation at an increasing rate, and unless this company climbed on the bandwagon, he claimed it would be left behind.

One of the older directors thanked him at the end of the talk and then proceeded to give him a short history lesson on the organisation, starting in 1780s when two of his very distant ancestors had set up the company. Their method of working for the first 25 years was to outsource most of their operations, acting as a final assembler and marketeer. They even outsourced the bookkeeping and accounts. They did not call it 'outsourcing', however: to them it was sub-contracting. The director did not disagree that the concept was a very valid one, to be considered carefully and continuously, but only disagreed that it was 'new'!

That, of course, is the irony of this aspect of flexibility, and a source of criticism – it is a step back in time to an age when labour supply was plentiful, to be used and dispensed with as required. It is a reversal of the process for the last 100 years where companies, as they grow organically, have taken in-house nearly all the operations and services that they previously bought in. This process reached its pinnacle in Henry Ford's Detroit works, where iron control was exercised in a completely integrated structure over every aspect of activity through the employment contract. Now, the movement is towards vertical disintegration together with flexible contractual relationships. The thinking is that organisations should concentrate on their core activities, which build competitive edge and add shareholder value. Everything else is 'context': tasks that should be carried out efficiently by whoever does them best, inside or outside the organisation.

Today's definition of outsourcing could be best summed up as where an organisation passes the provision of a service or execution of a task previously undertaken in-house, to a third party to perform on its behalf. This distinguishes it from subcontracting, which is generally work that has not customarily been carried on in-house. However, it can be stretched to include franchising arrangements and 'linked' subcontracting, where the organisation helps a group of employees set up as independent or semi-independent contractors. In France, for example, the practice of 'essimage' or 'spin-off' outsourcing allows employees to create their own independent business activities linked to their former firm, which in turn supports them by training or establishing preferential customer–supplier agreements.

Evidence from a number of surveys indicates that some forms of outsourcing have become much more common since the 1980s. One current estimate of the value of outsourced contracts in the UK is around £5 billion. Catering provision, security, payroll, logistics and cleaning have all been hived off from mainstream activity and outsourced to specialist providers. Where the work has gone abroad, it is called 'offshoring'.

The increasing opportunities to outsource provide organisations with much increased flexibility of operations, including staffing decisions. In the Institute of Management guide on *Outsourcing*, Mike Johnson (1997) lists the following top strategic reasons to go down this route:

- *Improve business focus:* outsourcing lets the company focus on broader issues while having operational details assumed by an outside expert. It avoids siphoning off huge amounts of management resources and attention on non-core activities.

- *Access to world-class capabilities:* outsourcing providers, especially in the IT field, can bring extensive, world-wide knowledge and experience giving access to new technology, career opportunities to employees who may transfer to the provider, and competitive advantage through expanded skills.

- *Accelerated re-engineering benefits:* This lets the provider, one that has already re-engineered to world-class standards, take over the process.

- *Sharing risks:* A co-operative venture with a provider can halve the risks.

There are two distinct strands in the current direction of outsourcing. First, there is the move by organisations in the private sector to use outsourcing as means to achieve cost and competitive advantage; second, there have been political moves by the Labour government to compel market testing (and thereby a degree of outsourcing) through the legislation which introduced best value, replacing the original Conservative government-inspired compulsory competitive tendering (CCT). Further developments in the early 2000s introduced comprehensive performance assessments (CPAs) to judge whether government departments and local authorities' in-house or outsourced systems were operating effectively. The aim behind these political moves has been to introduce competition into the public sector and to replicate the benefits reputedly achieved in the private sector.

Has outsourcing been successful?

Very mixed results have been reported. In an extensive survey by the University of Sheffield (2004), the following responses were obtained from 564 companies active in outsourcing:

Entirely achieved the objectives set	10 per cent
Achieved a lot of objectives set	26 per cent
Moderately successful in achieving its objectives	30 per cent
Achieved a few of the objectives set	9 per cent
Entirely failed to achieve its objectives	25 per cent.

The main reasons for the large failure rate were that high cost savings expectations were not realised, together with problems in managing the contract and service/quality levels. A survey by PA Consulting Group in 1998 showed a similar level of failure, with the bulk of the respondents reporting only a 'fairly neutral outcome' (Lonsdale and Cox 1998).

One of the most successful players in outsourcing, Capita, has won contracts totalling many billions of pounds, including a 10-year agreement worth £500 million to administer television licensing in 2002. However, in addition to many smoothly running and successful contracts, it has been associated with some high-profile disasters, such as the Criminal Records Bureau teacher-vetting scheme, London Borough of Lambeth's housing benefit scheme and the fraud-ridden individual learning account (ILO) scheme. In Lambeth's case, benefit claims were taking an average of 87 days to process instead of the agreed legal target of 14 days. Failures were a result of many factors including a poor relationship between the parties, high turnover of staff, cost-cutting measures by Capita and inadequate staff training throughout the contracts (Hammond 2002).

Offshoring has become a very hot issue in recent years, especially in terms of the call centre and back-office activity moving to the Indian subcontinent. Although there are enormous cost savings to be made in these moves, there are also risks. These include the insufficient knowledge of call centre operators in areas such as complex UK financial products (mortgages and pensions) and even British geography. Such failings risk a loss of customer confidence (People Management 2003).

The drive to outsource in the private sector

The competitive environment caused many organisations to look carefully at their cost and employment base to try to eliminate the activities in which they should not be involved. The general justifications for strategic decisions in this area have chiefly been:

- greater ability to focus on the core activities bringing competitive advantage
- cost saving
- improved service and flexibility in business activities
- security aspects.

Focus on core activities

'Our managers have enough to do without having to worry about managing cleaning, maintenance or the drains' reported an executive of a medium-sized engineering company in our survey. There has been a clear movement, beginning in the mid-1980s and picking up speed during the recession of the early 1990s, for organisations to restructure and de-layer, reducing sharply their managerial and supervisory staff numbers. Although tied up with cost reduction, the strategic direction has been to concentrate on mainstream activities and eliminating marginal areas, and become 'focused'.

British Airways took this policy to the extreme in the 1990s, looking at every activity to see if it could be outsourced. The airline's core activity is regarded as flying passengers, not providing their meals, moving their baggage or providing their security. All of these are ancillary activities that can be put out to tender if suitable contracts can be negotiated. In 1997, BA transferred 85 per cent of its ground fleet services staff (415 employees) to outsource provider Ryder under a five-year deal. The airline could then concentrate on building its flight network, increasing its reliability and serving its customers. It awarded contracts to a small but very flexible and customer-oriented organisation, the Astron group, for printing and other services (see Case study 9).

Cost savings

The recent perceived growth in outsourcing began when large organisations examined the more traditional areas of cleaning, catering and office services, and saw that smaller organisations with few overhead costs

Case study 9: Outsourcing to the Astron group

The Astron group used to be called a jobbing printer, but this scarcely describes the variety of outsourced contracts that it operates from four sites in the Hertfordshire/Huntingdon/Cambridge area. It employs around 300 permanent employees, but added to this number are around 300–400 'associates' who work a variety of hours when required.

To take an example, British Airways awarded the company a five-year contract to produce all its printed literature in the late 1990s. This activity used to be in-house, like so many of British Airways' operations, but a review in the 1990s of its core businesses persuaded the organisation that printing was not at the core. This was despite the fact that planes cannot take off unless the correct flight documentation is delivered to the plane on time by Astron staff.

Working times

At Letchworth, the flight documentation and numerous other sets of printed literature are produced by teams of employees roughly split 60:40 permanent to associate. The amount of work is unpredictable as British Airways and other customers often give the organisation only 24 hours to complete a job. For this reason, the working hours are between 6:00 and 22:00, plus a full Saturday. Permanent employees work 150 hours over a four-week period but their times of work are not fixed. A week in advance the amount of work available is indicated, and the teams plus the team leaders organise themselves to be available to cover the work. The additional staffing needed is made up from associates, who are called in to fill the gaps. Overtime is worked only rarely when there is a severe bottleneck of work emanating from a series of contracts or a rash of sickness. It is not uncommon for employees to complete their 150 hours in three weeks and then to have the fourth week off. By the same token, a change in plan from a customer can mean that some of the permanent staff do not work for three or four days at the start of the month.

The associates

The Associates are a mixture of people who, for a variety of reasons, only make themselves available for a limited number of hours. They may have caring responsibilities for children or older relatives, which bring regular and special time commitments; they may be students who are available in evenings after school or on certain days while they are at the local college. Many of them have family connections at the site, with many extended families working at different times. From the organisation's viewpoint, it is important to recruit associates for whom the variety of hours is not a disadvantage. They first needed to be quite clear on both the nature of the contract – that they usually have little notice and the hours of work for which they will be invited can vary – and the importance of the work they will carry out. No matter their background, they are key employees who must understand the importance of the deadlines and the need to satisfy customers.

The skill levels required are not high, except for certain specialist printing operations, but a careful responsible attitude is vital to ensure the work is completed at the right quality levels. Associates are persuaded from their first day that their work can be a 'show-stopper'. If it is not completed right, the plane will not take off.

Team working and training

Team working is a vital ingredient in the success of the operation. The employees are genuinely empowered to organise the work themselves, to share the hours in a constructive and co-operative way, and to share also the responsibility for getting the work completed on time.

Training is competence-driven. Associates are taught a selection of jobs so that they can slot into whichever position is required that day or week. When they become competent at the set of jobs so they can carry them out without supervision, they move onto a higher rate of pay. The final stage is to promote permanent staff onto a higher grade when they are capable of training other staff. When any permanent positions become available, they are offered to associates.

Conclusion

Astron's chief executive encouraged this way of working from a early stage in the company's expansion. He explained:

> *I want committed people to work for me and I really do not mind how many hours they work. There has to be this mutual trust*

> *associated with the empowered workforce. I know they will make mistakes that they may not make if they were under tight supervision, but I also know they would not use their initiative at vital times if somebody was standing over them. In the competitive world of outsourcing, we cannot afford tight supervision – we need to reach the high standards demanded by British Airways and Rank through the intelligence and commitment of our employees who see what needs to be done and just do it.*

Source: author's research.

could provide a far cheaper service than the in-house service which had to carry high overheads and pay rates often locked into a job-evaluated system.

Contractors can put forward a more competitive price for a number of reasons:

- They become expert in their field and know how to achieve high levels of productivity.

- They operate under flexible staffing levels, where part-time and temporary work is the convention to meet the needs of the many businesses for which they work.

- Employees can be moved from one contract to another as required to meet swings in demand.

- The culture of the organisation is one that is customer-oriented so employees become used to short-term changes and variety in working hours.

- Service innovation arises naturally from an organisation geared to meeting the whims of demanding customers, and such innovations can be transferred across many small contracts.

- Pay and rewards are much more likely to be performance-based.

- Benefits tend to be less generous, particularly in the areas of pension and private health insurance.

A further advantage of outsourcing which is attractive to accountants is that all the costs are variable, as the investment costs are borne by the contractor.

Improved service and flexibility

On a simple level, providers of outsourced services for, say, cleaning or catering know they will lose business and reputation if they do not provide the level of service their clients want and expect. Their contract and the jobs of their employees depend on this. Contracts are generally constructed to allow a degree of flexibility to reflect changing business circumstances, such as an increase or decrease in warehousing facilities.

On another level, getting up to date in rapidly advancing technology can be an expensive business, so there is an argument that organisations do best to leave this to a specialist company and simply use their services. Such companies are likely to be small, highly skilled and nimble, this being the core activity on which they are focused. Should a better, state-of-the-art service be offered by a competitor, the organisation can switch at the end of the contract period.

Malcolm Howard, head of business development for Accenture HR Services, has explained that flexibility is top of the outsourcing priority list for most organisations. The more imaginative companies are looking for flexibility in service relationship as well as reduced cost. It adds capability and allows companies to scale up their operations quickly – and scale them back just as fast. (Smethurst 2003b, p6)

Where logistical aspects are involved, using a nationwide provider generally gives better methods of access than trying to achieve the result in-house.

Security aspects

Throughout the 1980s, companies moved to outsource part or all of their logistical operations. Back in the 1970s when most lorry fleets were in-house, a strike brought most companies rapidly to a halt and the settlements reached caused considerable financial headaches. It was in the interests of both supplier and customer that deliveries would remain secure in any possible strike situation. Organisations that were non-union, or where unions were benign, were especially successful in winning contracts. Political support was given to this movement by the legislation outlawing secondary picketing.

Outsourcing in the public sector

One of the most controversial innovations of the 1980s was the introduction of CCT in the public sector, a process now called 'market testing' or 'best value'. In a openly ideological move to eliminate 'municipal socialism', with its emphasis on public accountability, democratic ownership and mass provision and service for those in need, a batch of legislation was passed (the Local Government Planning and Land Act 1980, and the Local Government Acts of 1988 and 1992) to force local authorities to put their services out to tender in the market place. It began with routine highway and buildings maintenance, then extended to manual services such as refuse collection, street cleaning and lighting. Finally administrative services came into the firing line, including IT, personnel, facilities management and legal provision. An example in the property field is shown in Case study 10.

Overall, the evidence (chiefly from the Audit Commission) has been strongly in favour of success. Substantial savings have been achieved, often in the order of 20 per cent or more, and quality has been maintained or improved. These findings have been questioned within local authorities, where issues of comparative quality and monitoring costs have been raised, but few deny that the public has benefited from the initiative. So successful had the process become that the policy was continued by the Labour government from 1997 onwards with changes only at the margins. In fact, the development and encouragement of public–private partnerships (PPPs) has been at the heart of many large-scale funding operations in the public sector. It is estimated that the public sector outsourcing market is worth over £10 billion a year in its various forms. An independent report (Accenture 2003) found that the UK public sector has the most mature outsourcing market in the world, with a sophisticated approach to transforming services, rather than just cutting costs.

Case study 10: Outsourcing property development at Surrey County Council

Surrey County Council has entered into a partnership arrangement with Equion to develop the county's proposals to help streamline its office portfolio, develop a new County Hall and take over the management of its offices on a 30-year contract. The aims were to help save £26 million over the long term by reducing the costs of offices and office services, create a more flexible working environment for staff, and provide a better centralised office facility, with the financial risk taken on board by Equion.

Around 3–4,000 staff were affected by the development, including a number who transferred to Equion under TUPE arrangements.

Source: Surrey County Council internal documents.

External providers have not won all the contracts. The regular reports on contracts by the Employers Association show that direct service organisations (DSOs) have continued to win a majority, especially in areas such as sport and leisure management. However, winning was often at the price of fundamentally changing their ways of working to match the private-sector organisations they were bidding against. In street lighting, for example, flexible shifts have replaced fixed starting and stopping time, operatives carry out all lighting repairs and installations, rather than just concentrating on one area, and payment systems have reflected individual and team effort rather than a straight hourly wage plus regular overtime. The effect has been a more efficient force but at the expense of greatly reduced numbers. A 20 per cent saving has often arisen from 30 per cent fewer employees.

An interesting development throughout the process has been the monitoring of contracts, a factor which became included in the tender document from an early stage in its development. Complaints from the public have been counted and published, independent customer surveys commissioned, and warnings issued to the contractor (including the DSO where relevant) where the service has been found wanting. Prior to CCT, the public had to grin and bear any shortcomings, or attempt to exert political pressure through local councillors. It is now rare for the provider of a poor local authority service to survive for long, and early termination of contracts is not unknown. An example of this is Enfield Council in North London, where three major contracts for cleaning and catering in schools and at the civic centre had to be re-tendered following news that the DSO was effectively facing bankruptcy. The problem arose from a tribunal decision that the council had to reinstate national pay terms and conditions, which pushed up its costs by around £500,000 and made it impossible for the DSO to meet its financial targets under the contracts (Enfield Advertiser 1997).

Difficulties in the outsourcing process

Defining the contract

No contract is simple to formulate, but outsourcing services are more prone to difficulties, particularly where the level of service is defined. This is a key area because the contract is worthless unless there are opportunities to terminate it if quality is not sufficient. But how, for example, do you define a satisfactory level of catering service or ambulance service? Experience has provided measures that can be used, such as user surveys, but these can be time-consuming or expensive.

Subcontracting in the construction industry is strewn with examples where arguments over contract definition (in particular the issue of whether an item is an 'extra' or an integral part of the contract) finishes up in the courts or at costly arbitration. The same can apply in any outsourced activity.

Bureaucratic nightmare?

Under best value, contracts can almost literally weigh a ton. Contracts for street cleaning or grass verge cutting, even in a small authority, can be 600 pages long, and all the clauses need to be examined carefully by prospective providers. The contracts are this length for three reasons. First is the need to specify carefully the work that has to be done, how it is to be done and the detailed quality measures; second, the legal department will have recommended many additions to ensure that the contract is watertight; third, the complexity is sometimes designed to discourage many outside providers, especially smaller ones, giving the existing in-house providers a better chance to win the contract.

Contracts in the private sector are less likely to face such problems, but legal difficulties mean that contracts are tending to become more complex each year.

Losing control

Many organisations would be very pleased to lose control of cleaning or catering, but in more strategic areas (IT comes immediately to mind), there has to be a degree of hesitation before passing over these activities to an outsider. It is not just that security aspects are important, but the organisation's body of knowledge becomes reduced. In the future, should there be a need to reverse the decision, it may not be quite so easy to take the function back on board at the level of competence required. Organisations that have needed to do this have faced some severe management resourcing problems.

These arguments are well rehearsed with subcontracting activities in manufacturing, where vital R&D skills, experience and career opportunities can be lost if it is decided to outsource a major component. A lean organisation may become anorexic and miss vital opportunities that arise, often unexpectedly, if focused experts have been lost through outsourcing. Some argue that the problems get worse the longer the work is outsourced. This is because the provider progressively knows more about the organisation, while the expertise within the organisation deteriorates.

Another area where control is lost is in the actual employees working on the contract. Recruitment, discipline and termination are in the hands of the provider. The provider's employees may not share the values, commitment or enthusiasm that the organisation would ideally like, but possible action is limited unless controls in these areas are written into the contract.

Dealing with the provider

Employees may face some frustrations in dealing with an outside body in activities that concern them. This arises more in IT than in most other areas, since here the process of setting priorities in system development can be far more complex than when all the IT is managed in-house. It is also quite common for the outsourced service to be more tightly focused, so employees can be disappointed when making peripheral demands that used to be quickly met under the previous, less focused but user-friendly regime.

Maintaining the quality

Even if quality standards are agreed and measures are in place, it still remains a difficult situation if the provider does not meet those standards. If the activities were in-house, heads would roll and direct action could be taken, but this is more difficult to enforce with a contractor. Time-consuming negotiations need to take place, and if these fail to achieve results the only recourse is to terminate the contract after due notice, which can lead to expensive legal action. A number of local authorities have insisted on the provider putting up performance bonds which are forfeit if the performance does not meet the standard specified. For building cleaning alone, 170 CCT contracts incurred financial penalties in the second half of 1996 (LGMB 1996). More recently, Capital One withdrew from an offshoring arrangement with Wipro Spectramind in New Delhi after an internal audit of Indian workers showed certain aspects were not in keeping with standards and practices, while Dell and Lehmann Bros took their helpdesks back to the United States after customers complained about poor service from third-world subcontractors (Simms 2004).

Viability of provider

Providers may be flexible and nimble-footed in meeting the client's needs, but sometimes they fall over or simply disappear. In the six months to December 1996, 21 CCT contracts in the leisure sector were terminated as a result of two leisure companies going into receivership (LGMB 1996), and contracts with a further six private companies were terminated on similar grounds.

How will the employees react?

There was substantial disquiet in the early 2000s about the amount of work being outsourced abroad, especially in the field of IT and HR. Newspaper reports appeared weekly concerning back-office banking jobs, call centre work and HR administration being transferred to the Indian subcontinent, although this appears to have had little overall effect on UK employment in these areas, with the possible exception of specialist IT work. However, the threat of such transfer can have a salutary effect on the agreement of employees to changing processes and introducing economies.

The response of employees who have actually been involved in the outsourcing process has been more difficult to identify. Kessler, Coyle-Shapiro and Purcell (1999) studied one such case in detail, and found that employees had, in general, greater job satisfaction after they had been transferred with the work to another provider. A more pessimistic viewpoint emerged from a later study of two PPP contracts, one in the health sector and another in housing benefit claims (Hebson, Grimshaw and Marchington 2003). Here, the contractual relationships led to a clear weakening of traditional notions of managerial accountability, together with a 'vicious circle of monitoring and distrust between partner organisations, an intensification of work and extensive cost cutting' (p481).

Nor is the practice universally popular in America. IBM staff staged a massive demonstration in April 2004 against the organisation's focus on offshoring thousands of jobs to India, China and Brazil (Jacques and Lynch 2004). The company responded by setting up a US$25 million fund to help those affected to retrain and find jobs with IBM's partners.

Transferring employees

The rules come under the general banner of the Transfer of Undertakings (Protection of Employment) Regulations 1981 (TUPE), which implemented in the UK the European Union Acquired Rights Directive 1977. Recent interpretations of this legislation in both UK and in other EU countries have made it very difficult to understand, and presented some extreme operational difficulties. These are too complex to deal with in detail in this publication, so readers are referred to the sources given in the References. It must be said, however, that the interpretation of law in this area has the habit of changing rapidly and drastically.

Difficulties can arise because employees often have to transfer without a choice (although they retain the same terms and conditions for an extended period, usually at least six months), or are presented with the options of staying with the organisation but in a different role, transferring or taking redundancy. They need, and should expect, impartial advice, but this may not be forthcoming from the organisation, which will have its own agenda for individual employees. There are ethical dilemmas for personnel staff when it may be in the organisation's interest to persuade difficult or unsatisfactory employees to take redundancy or to transfer.

In February 2003 a new code of practice relating to contracts transferred in the public sector was introduced, which amended the TUPE regulations. The most important change is that new employees taken on after an outsourcing transfer of employees must have no less favourable terms than those of the TUPE-protected staff. This arose from union pressure against the existence of two-tier workforces, and was regarded as a disappointing climb-down by employers' associations.

Adding to the complexity of this whole area, an agreement was reached in 2003 to trial a working relationship under NHS private finance initiatives (PFIs), where employees who would normally be transferred to a private employer under TUPE can decide instead to stay employed by the NHS but be 'seconded' to the private employer. Their employment is governed by agreements set up in the PFI contract and priced into it, relating to such items as pension provision, disciplinary and grievance procedures (Marston, Learmond-Criqui and Holt 2003).

Outsourcing IT

There has been a rapid increase in the last five years in the outsourcing of computer services, including payroll activities. This has been a fascinating subject to observe, as IT departments have often been the most difficult to manage, with change occurring constantly and knife-edge investment decisions needed rapidly. The staffing has also been fraught with high turnover and security implications. Lacity, Hirschheim and Willcocks (1994) reported that the justification for outsourcing IT by one organisation was simply to eliminate a troublesome function and, by implication, relieve the senior executives of daily staffing and other crises.

Outsourcing HR

A CIPD survey in 2003 (Brown and Emmott 2003) concluded that the outsourcing of HR activities had been over-hyped. Only a quarter of participants had significantly increased their use of external providers in the previous three years, mostly in recruitment and training provision. In fact, a number of organisations were bringing services back in-house, and more provision was being pulled back to the centre, with increasing use of internal shared-service centres in support of more effective e-HR. There were a number of reports of shared services proving difficult, with cost overruns and systems problems.

Interestingly, on the same publication date it was reported that BP has brought its pension administration back in-house, bucking its 10-year trend towards large-scale outsourcing. Bruce Garner, BP's head of pensions, commented that:

> *BP's aim was to establish leading standards in customer service to scheme members and because of the size and complexity of the project (30 different schemes, 80,000 members) it could not be achieved by an external provider.*
>
> *(Brown and Emmott 2003)*

There is certainly evidence that larger organisations are moving towards the 'shared services' model of HR provision, where line managers access internal HR knowledge by contacting a centralised case centre or interrogating an intranet database of information. Certainly there may be more use of HR outsourcing, but it is likely that this will be restricted to administrative matters that do not immediately add value or are highly specialised, such as legal advice.

Reed Managed Services (2002) reported that the main problems in outsourcing HR related to what it called 'cultural dissonance': essentially a lack of match with the culture and systems of the organisation, which aroused considerable suspicion and distrust among employees. Successful deals are centred around a high degree of trust between the parties and a dislike of legal ring-fencing. 'Once you get to the stage of involving the legal profession, you are half-way to failure,' reported John Ainsby, instructor for QA, which provides training services in managing outsourcing (Rodgers 2002).

Two very different examples of outsourcing HR are shown in case studies 11 and 12.

Conclusion

There is a view among some employee representatives that the whole area of outsourcing has been introduced with a different agenda. It is a way to frighten employees by threatening to outsource activities so that performance improves. There may be little or no real intention to actually transfer the work,

Case study 11: Bruton Knowles, insourcing HR

When the personnel manager of Bruton Knowles, a firm of chartered surveyors employing 220 staff, left in the mid-1990s, the organisation decided against a replacement. Instead it brought in an HR manager, Alison Mellis, from consultancy firm Ellis Hayward on a fee basis. This arrangement ensured a higher level of expertise and a degree of independent viewpoint. Her work has been a mix of strategic initiatives, including change management, and ensuring effective day-to-day HR administration, using internal resources. The combination of cost-effective service and quality expertise has proved to provide a far better service than a traditional, employed personnel department.

Source: Pickard (1998).

Case study 12: Liverpool Victoria, outsourcing HR

In 2000, the Personal Investment Authority handed out severe criticism of Liverpool Victoria's (LV) HR policies, especially recruitment and training, and the organisation was punished with a £900,000 fine. Its reaction was to start afresh and outsource all its HR, together with facilities and IT, with a view to achieving much improved customer service and top-quartile products.

Six months was spent in defining what was wanted and establishing the borderlines between HR strategy and policy, which would remain in-house, and the remainder of the HR function, which would be outsourced. There was disappointment with the quality of the tenders, with most not understanding what LV required, but Hays met the requirements, and started work in April 2001. It was another six months before the contract was signed. The time was taken up with negotiation on the contract detail, especially performance measures, and the process of transfer of staff. A number went to the new customer-contact centre in Leicester, some distance from LV's base in Bournemouth. There was a very steep learning curve for new employees at this centre.

Although the viewpoint in 2003 was that Hays was 'good on some things, adequate on others and not quite good enough on very few things,' the overall picture is one of success, with savings achieved by LV and profit on the contract by Hays.

Source: Smethurst (2003a).

but the perceived threat is sufficient to drive through changes that would otherwise prove difficult to achieve. Thus employers manage to change working practices, hours of work, terms and conditions and whole sets of attitudes not through the threat of loss of business through competition, but by an implied or actual threat of outsourcing.

TEMPORARY EMPLOYEES AND SHORT-TERM CONTRACTS

Meeting the organisation's need to respond flexibly to the ever-changing pattern of demand

Flexible practices in the workplace often reflect the calculated decisions (or sometimes just whims or impulses) of consumers – that collection of complex decisions we make each day as to when and where to shop and what to buy at what price in what quantities. Unpredictability has sharply increased from a business viewpoint, because the choice to consumers has never been so great. They have an increasing ability to shop around through access to telephones, cars and the Internet, and there is increasing competition to provide convenient shopping opportunities through extended opening hours, telesales and sales recording systems.

In employment terms, this uncertainty in current and medium-term activities has caused many employers to extend the use of temporary employment policies. These have taken a variety of forms associated with the new concept of complementary workers, the main ones being the more extensive use of short-term contracts, casual and temporary agency staff. A number of organisations have moved a stage further by setting up in-house contracts. So great has been the need for temporary staff in the NHS that the government has set up a dedicated national agency, NHS Professionals, with an annual budget of £11 million, to provide all types of agency staff. It has gradually been taking over many hospital trust 'bank' schemes, and estimates the overall cost saving made through such arrangements to be 5–10 per cent.

The label 'casual worker' or 'temp' conveys an image of employees of no great importance to the organisation – mostly unskilled, generally very short-term, and certainly of low status. There are signs that this is all changing. Complementary workers are employees who are in a non-permanent capacity with the host organisation, to which they provide services either directly or through a third party, and they are starting to make a much more sizeable contribution to the business performance of their host organisations.

This section starts with information relating to the current state of temporary and short-term employment. Then complementary employment is explained and discussed, together with the use of agency labour and the legal implications. There a number of short case studies.

Current extent of temporary work

It is estimated that around 6.5 per cent of employees work on temporary contracts, a total of just over 1.8 million (Labour Market Trends 2003). This proportion has risen steadily since the 1980s, when the figure was closer to 5 per cent, reflecting the drive by employers towards retaining a higher degree of numeric flexibility. Of these temporary employees:

- 46 per cent are on fixed-term contracts
- 33 per cent are on casual or seasonal contracts
- 16 per cent are agency temps
- 5 per cent work from home or are on zero hours contracts.

The proportion of agency temps has risen substantially since 1990, while those on zero contracts have fallen, mostly as a result of a change in the legal status of zero hours contracts.

IDS (2000) reported that a good proportion of these so-called temporary jobs lasted a very long time. Thirty-eight per cent of casual/seasonal arrangements, 33 per cent of fixed-term contracts and one in 12 agency placements lasted two years or more, although the majority of jobs in all cases did not exceed a year.

Not unsurprisingly, 60 per cent of temporary jobs are in professional, technical, clerical and administrative areas. Compared with the rest of Europe, however, the UK still has a very low percentage of temporary employees. For example, 32 per cent of all employment in Spain is temporary, and even in France, Germany and Japan it reaches 10 per cent. Only Belgium and Italy have a level around that of the UK. Most countries, except Japan, Belgium and the UK, have a roughly equal division between males and females in temporary employment.

Locating temporary employees

In recent years, the number of sources of temporary employees has increased greatly:

- *Students:* the number of full-time HE students in 2002 was 1.25 million, an increase of 13 per cent since 1997, and a figure that is increasing at a rate of 3 or 4 per cent a year. Because of the elimination of grants and introduction of fees, nearly all students have to work. Rates of pay are often at or just above the national minimum wage. In fact, over 12 per cent of all temporary employees have degrees or equivalent qualifications.

- *Older employees downshifting:* there has been a strong tendency in recent years for employees to leave their employment before retirement age due to generous pension arrangements for long-serving employees or through enforced redundancy or a decline in health. This has been especially true for men, when the participation rate for those aged 50–65 has dropped to less than 70 per cent.

A good proportion of these need the income from temporary work, but there are also a minority who look to work because they are fitter than previous generations and welcome the activity, sociability, and frankly the time taken up by a temporary position. In fact, there is strong evidence that the trend towards lower participation has been starting to reverse since 2000, and that many are coming out of enforced early retirement or looking much more actively for employment. Much of this is a result of the actual and anticipated reduction in pension benefits, but it is also because employers have redesigned jobs to allow older people to take them up.

- *Overseas sources:* the growing number of overseas visitors, especially those coming to study or on short-term visas, has provided a large source for basic temporary work.

- *Women returners:* the participation rate for women returning to work after having a family has increased substantially. According to Labour Force Survey data in 2005, 36 per cent of the 900,000 female employees were happy to stay working as temporaries and did not want a permanent job.

- *IT staff:* in the 1990s, many IT employees saw that working on a succession of well-paid short-term contracts had advantages over a permanent position. In those heady days, deals were often struck whereby current employment was terminated and replaced by a short-term contract with an attractive terminal performance-related bonus. In the more realistic 2000s, a large number of IT staff still remain on fixed contracts, but for a good many, this is because they cannot find a permanent position in the slimmed-down industry.

Reasons for using temporary labour

The four main reasons given by organisations for employing temporary employees are covering the absence of permanent employees, coping with fluctuations in workload, completing specific or specialist projects, and minimising redundancies where changes to working practices are anticipated (IDS 2000).

Contrary to the commonly held view that most temporary jobs are low-paid and low-skill, highly skilled and often highly paid professional jobs in specialised fields are often filled by temporary employees. Around 60 per cent of staff on short-term contracts are in the professional and managerial sector.

Types of contracts

For individual workers, contracts are mostly short-term, but examples are now arising of agency providers who are treating their workers as employees and entering into long-term relationships with them. Manpower, with 300 UK offices and operations in 67 countries, is the largest example of an agency that directly and wholly employs all the temporary staff it places, although the direction of day-to-day activities is handled by its customers. All staff enjoy 20 days of paid holidays after a qualifying period, and there are schemes for sickness and maternity pay, together with life and personal accident insurance.

The nature of the contract between the agency and customer also varies greatly. Where the provider has a key role in helping the organisation improve productivity and reduce costs, as in the Manpower–Xerox case (see case study 13), the responsibilities are for providing a total service involving many aspects of output, quality and time-managed service delivery within the customer's manufacturing or service environment.

Consulting agreements are linked to negotiated outcomes, while the contract for a simple temporary assignment is based on providing a body in place over a period of time with a degree of quality and skills expectations.

Relationship with supplier

There are crucial differences here. Providing temporary staff can mean a very simple arrangement, such as a short-term contract for seasonal employees. Contracting for a total in-plant or outsourcing operation will certainly be long-term, complex, and more importantly strategic. The relationship will allow the company to respond quickly to changing market conditions without the ultimate responsibility for redeploying staff. A strategic relationship implies a close liaison on strategic resourcing plans arising out of the client company's long-term strategic plan.

Case study 13: Working partnership: Manpower and Xerox

In 1999, one of Xerox's strategic plans was to reduce the company's operational costs while maintaining a high level of customer service in the competitive photocopying market. To meet these objectives, Xerox wanted a strategic partner to assist in dealing with customer requests to fix faulty equipment across the UK. Xerox's key requirement was for a quality supplier of staffing solutions that could enhance its own internal capability for a fixed price, provide skilled staff and deliver a national solution, with the ability to flex the workforce according to customer demand.

Manpower set up a new staffing infrastructure within Xerox, consisting of HR managers, support managers and a team of 100 skilled engineers nationwide, which had risen to 350 by 2004. Manpower managed the recruitment and training process for field engineers and schedulers, who were a mix of temporary and permanent employees. Xerox's call centre customer call routing system was integrated with a tracking and fulfillment system to schedule engineers to deliver the required work across different customer sites.

The outcome of the partnership was a reduction in costs of between 15 per cent and 18 per cent and an improvement of 10 per cent in productivity. As Sandy Menzies, Xerox's service partner and logistics manager, explained:

> *By partnering with Manpower, Xerox has been able to effectively transition its highly seasonal workload to a more flexible workforce, gaining both productivity and cost per fix benefits, whilst maintaining the high quality of performance to meet our customers' demands. But the biggest benefit is for our customers, who now see an engineer more quickly.*

Source: Manpower UK Ltd.

Skills and knowledge

Contracting and consulting work almost inevitably means the supplier providing a high degree of skill and knowledge. There may, on the other hand, be very little skill involved in the labour provided for routine clerical work. Increasingly, however, the levels of skill required in complementary workforces is rising. This is particularly true with in-plant and outsourced operations, where people with a collection of specialist skills (IT, engineering, technical, professional and so on) work alongside those with the more general skills of management and supervision.

Recognising this, a number of providers are increasingly concentrating on improving their skills banks. Manpower has developed a full set of office automation and IT skills training modules (Skillware and Techtrack), and encourages all its staff to accumulate skills ranging from basic word processing and spreadsheets to higher-level skills for IT professionals such as in systems and database design. At the heart of the training is an effective skills assessment system which aims to guarantee the quality of the skills. Much of the training programme is in the form of an online university, available 24 hours a day, which allows employees to receive training and gain qualifications in areas that they feel they need developing.

There are several reasons for Manpower to invest substantially in a temporary labour force:

- A growing proportion of its labour force is no longer 'temporary' in the strict sense of the word. Individuals can work on one assignment for an extended period, stretching to many years, or they can move regularly between assignments. The payback period on training is the same as for any 'permanent' employee in an organisation.

- The more skilled the workforce, the greater the resources the organisation has to offer – it is, in fact, all it has to offer – so in a world that respects quality, employee assets have to be seen to be high quality. (One of the generic training skills, incidentally, is customer care techniques, and Manpower aims to have all its staff to achieve this module.)

- The skills give the agency itself flexibility. When work falls off at one organisation, employees with the right skills (or the right learning mindset) can be switched to another suitable assignment.

A final caveat is warranted at this point. Not all employers are moving to increase their temporary workforce. In 1999, the National Exhibition Centre in Birmingham moved from using 80 casual staff in its box office to 34 permanent staff on an annualised hours basis. This improved the customer service considerably, with far less absence and staff turnover. Research by the Joseph Rowntree Foundation (1999) indicated a drop in employee enthusiasm for casual and temporary work, and organisations were finding it more difficult to attract, retain and motivate such staff. Several organisations in the financial services and education sectors had reduced their usage considerably and moved towards offering better work–life balance benefits to reduce staff turnover.

Interim management

Another comparatively new subsector in this field is interim management, which is estimated to have an annual turnover of £200 million and to be growing by 25 per cent annually. Around 10,000 managers work at a senior level, summoned at short notice to perform a specific task for anything from a few weeks to a year or more. As downsizing and de-layering have taken their toll, organisations remain unwilling to start increasing their permanent headcount, so they look elsewhere for management skills to run short-term assignments. Most managers involved are over 45, and have had exposure to a number of managerial situations. Their willingness to take on these assignments is related to the difficulty at their age in obtaining permanent positions.

Organisation use interim managers in four situations.

- In project work where they have no in-house expertise, such as investigating a new market place, perhaps Scotland or Ireland, or helping install a new budgetary control system.

- When there is a truly temporary position, as when two companies are merging and one finance director leaves four months before the actual merger takes place.

Case study 14: Interim HR position at the London Borough of Newham

Jackie Atchinson took up an interim position as head of HR for housing at the London Borough of Newham in April 2002, at the time of a substantial review and merger of HR departments. Her prime objective was to raise the profile of HR and sell its services to the internal client base, and she saw one of the main benefits of the appointment as that her input was based on what was best for the organisation, rather than her own career aspirations. This led to a more trusting relationship, although quick results were expected for her stay of less than a year. She achieved almost immediate success through implementing better guidance to managers on attendance and long-term sickness: for example, this led to 24 long-term absent employees returning to work. Her greatest challenge was to gain the support of the team when they knew she would only be *in situ* for a short time.

Source: *People Management* (2002).

- At a higher level, a 'company doctor' may be required plus a small team to try to turn round an ailing business over a limited period of time.

- There are a growing number of cases of short-term senior vacancies as a result of maternity leave.

The advantages are clear. The managers are immediately effective (often being over-qualified), and can make way when their assignment is finished for a less qualified and cheaper manager who will simply run the operation. Interim managers can be expensive, with the cost in the range of £300 to £1,500 a day, but they are still generally cheaper and more controllable than a batch of consultants. Interim managers are also committed, working full-time on one assignment, and needing good results to be hired for the next one. They can also provide objective advice, being outside the political loop of the organisation, as was the situation for Jackie Atchinson (see Case study 14).

Legal issues in temporary employment

Drafting and using fixed-term contracts

An organisation has to take care when drafting fixed-term contracts. One of the key reasons for implementing such a contract is to ensure that there are no legal liabilities when the contract reaches its termination point. This is a notoriously complex part of the law, with different rulings to exclude redundancy claims and unfair dismissal claims, so the policy and wording has to be quite clear on this and other points.

Some key points are detailed here, but only in outline, and you are recommended to read a legal text carefully before entering into these contracts:

- If the contract is going to extend beyond two years, it should include a waiver clause concerning redundancy rights. The waiver clause could read: 'The employee agrees to waive any redundancy rights which may otherwise arise on the expiry and non-renewal of this contract.'

- Under the Fixed-Term Employees (Prevention of Less Favourable Treatment) Regulations 2002, employees on fixed-term contracts must not be treated less favourably than comparable permanent employees, including pay and benefits. There is also a maximum period of four years for a succession of fixed-term contracts, and such staff have the right to be informed of available vacancies.

- The Employment Act 1999 prohibited the use of waiver clauses relating to unfair dismissal claims for employees working under fixed-term contracts.

- Either make the termination date quite clear in the documentation (do not rely on word of mouth on this point), or if it is a performance or task contract, pinpoint the end by including a clause such as: 'The contract will terminate on the date on which the project completion certificate is signed' or 'The contract will end automatically when the budgeted funds for the programme are exhausted.'

- If terminal bonuses are involved, make quite clear the conditions that are attached, such as the measure of the minimum productivity and quality levels and how they are measured, the cost parameters and any other key features. Unless these are clearly laid down, the bonuses may well be a source of argument or even legal action.

- Do not try to rely on a series of short-term contracts to avoid employees claiming unfair dismissal or redundancy. In *Pfaffinger v City of Liverpool*, where a college lecturer had worked under term-time only contracts for some years and then left over a disputed change of pay, the court decided that he had accumulated service sufficiently to be able to claim redundancy.

- Ensure you insert a clause allowing either party to give notice of termination of the short-term contract, or should circumstances change and you no longer need the employee, you will be saddled with the obligation to pay salary for the whole of the outstanding period.

Are agency workers employees?

Despite a number of recent cases, the status of a temporary person working through an agency is still not clear. Until 1995, it was thought that people operating via an agency but not employed by that agency were self-employed because there was no obligation to provide work (although agencies, by law, have to deduct tax and national insurance). However, in *McMeechan v Secretary of State for Employment* (1995 EAT), the tribunal decided that McMeechan was an employee of the agency after considering all the terms and conditions of the contract, principally the degree of control exercised by the agency, even though his contract specified that he was self-employed.

However, in *Dacas v Brooke Street Bureau* (Court of Appeal 2004), Dacas had been kept on by the hiring company for more than a year and the court found that Dacas then became an employee of that company. It has to be said that the position is not completely clear at the time of writing.

Other difficult issues to consider

- Temporary employees can find it difficult to enter into a commitment to the organisation, to get involved in longer-term projects or social relationships.

- Financial planning becomes less easy for employees, especially over pensions, mortgages, children's education and holidays.

- Use of short-term staff can affect team-building in the organisation, as managers and permanent staff were less willing to provide key team posts for temporary employees or to give them the necessary training.

- Groups of employees on short-term contracts spread a culture of uncertainty in the organisation. If there have been redundancies, further rounds of job-cuts may be expected, and permanent employees may be uneasy as they wait for the axe to fall again. The culture is often associated with cynical viewpoints from permanent staff.

- The benefits are considered overall to be heavily weighted towards the employer, which leads to an overall concept of unfairness, particularly where the use of short-term contracts is seen as a strategic and semi-permanent arrangement.

- Trade unions in the service sector also campaign, not unexpectedly, against temporary employees. BIFU, the banking and insurance union, has estimated that there are 10,000 temporary and casual workers in the financial sector, which is a sign of chronic staff under-funding and is a specific strategy to create new, cheaper and more insecure forms of working.

Key factors in using complementary workers

Deciding the strategy

One point is clear from the beginning: to use complementary workers as a cost-cutting exercise alone is unlikely to succeed. As well as having a demotivating and divisive effect upon both permanent and complementary staff, it would be regarded by all concerned as a short-term process. Strategy calls for longer-term goals, and an effective flexibility strategy is crucial. For American Express, complementary workers are used to help the process of changing and consolidating services at a central site and supporting new products. The company is able to see how successful a new product is in the early days without over-committing valuable and limited human resources. For NatWest, complementary employees have been used to help set up and run telephone banking and other operations that take place outside the traditional 09:00 to 17:00 banking hours, rather than to change the culture and terms and conditions of existing staff.

Terms and conditions

Agency staff (as opposed to fixed-term contract staff) are often paid different rates from permanent employees doing the same job. In the original draft of the EU Agency Workers Directive, employers were forced to offer temporary workers the same employment conditions from day one, and the same rates of pay after a six-week qualifying period. This has been staunchly opposed by the British government, which wants a one-year qualifying period, and the EU ministers failed to agree on this issue at a summit in June 2003. In April 2005, this proposed directive was blocked by a minority of Member States and little progress is expected over the next two years. However, you need to keep up to date with this important set of negotiations.

Regulations took effect in April 2004 in respect of the arrangement where agency employees are offered permanent employment with the organisation with which they were placed. Before a posting with the company starts, companies, agencies and workers are free to reach agreement on the terms governing fees or the length of assignment that best suit their own wishes and circumstances. Only if terms are not agreed, the regulations impose a quarantine period that must pass before workers are free to take up a permanent post. These range for 14 weeks if the posting lasts a day to eight weeks if the posting lasts for more than six weeks.

Assessing the training and learning implications

As the economy moves steadily towards a low unemployment base, the issue of skills availability will become crucial. It is essential to agree informal contracts with temporary employees (whether directly or agency employed), and with the agency, which specify the training required to reach the skills levels and quality targets in the business plan. The division of training responsibility between the company and the agency is a key part of that contract.

A second feature is the creation of the learning environment. It is not easy to encourage employees to become interested and motivated to develop their formal and informal skills when their employment is on a limited basis, but many are now starting to realise that the variety of work experiences provide varied learning opportunities that can be valuable on their CV.

Differentiate or integrate?

Should temporary employees be distinguished from permanent employees in the work place? Since the Fixed-Term Employees Regulations 2002 came into force, any variation in pay and benefits has been very difficult to justify, except in isolated cases. For example, a permanent employee might have a company car, but an employee on a three-month contract might not be given a car because the costs are too high and other forms of transport are available. Each case needs to be examined on its merits. There are strong arguments for integrating temporary employees firmly into the business, inviting them to social events, and including them in all communication and consultation exercises.

Selecting the agency

Since the Deregulation and Contracting-Out Act 1995, agencies no longer need to be registered. There is self-regulation through the Federation of Recruitment and Employment Services (FRES), which has recently reviewed its code of practice and disciplinary procedure. With an estimated 15,000 agencies and an annual turnover exceeding £3 billion, it is important to work with a creditable organisation. FRES operate an arbitration service for clients and job-seekers.

It is clearly necessary to choose a supplier that has the experience an organisation needs at the level it needs, and one that will share the same expectations about the development of the relationship. For example, if an organisation is moving down the road of greater outsourcing and the use of complementary employees, the agency will need to be comfortable about accommodating the increased activities and responsibilities this strategy will demand.

Where there are a large number of agency-employed staff, the role of the HR department may alter, as it takes on the role of advisor and co-ordinator but is no longer responsible for delivering day-to-day solutions.

CONCLUSION

In this chapter, a selection of flexibility initiatives by employers have been detailed and analysed. In many cases, we have seen that the requirements for quality service, responsiveness to change and adaptability to meet technological developments have met with employee enthusiasm. Increasing skills, working to non-standard annualised hours, and working to a succession of highly paid interesting contracts can match employees' requirements very well, especially at certain times in their career and lifestyle.

However, there are also some drawbacks for employees, especially associated with outsourcing and temporary employment, where the balance sheet can be drawn up firmly in the employer's favour. Getting everybody to sign up for all the initiatives is not easy, and remains a challenge for the HR professional.

In Chapter 4, you will find a more detailed analysis of how to get all the systems to work effectively, from their strategic foundation to detailed advice on day-to-day operation.

3

The Brave New World: achieving flexibilisation by unlocking the potential of technology

INTRODUCTION

Technology touches almost every aspect of working life, and this is very much the case with flexible working. Technology can support and enable flexible working in a number of ways. Most obviously it enables working from flexible locations, it enhances communication opportunities, and cuts down response times to customers and colleagues. Effective HR managers these days needs to be fully aware of the technological issues relating to infrastructure, applications and business processes, if they are to get the most out of working flexibly.

However, technology will not answer all flexible working ills. Even the best thought-out technology will not disguise inadequacies in systems, processes and employee behaviours. Technology can be employed to change work routines, shorten processes and relocate operations, but this does not preclude the need for these routines and processes to be checked for appropriateness and relevance. In addition just because technology can be used to relocate work, this does not automatically mean it is the right thing to do.

HR expertise must now encompass a good understanding of the potential that technology gives us and the underlying principles that need to be in place before technology can be fully effective. It is no longer possible to leave technology issues to the 'techies', because as the saying goes, 'If you don't go to the tailors you can't expect a suit to fit.' IT experts are notorious for building systems that promise far greater functionality than users actually need, but omit the two or three basic functions they really need. The only way to avoid this is to be fully represented at the design and build phases, ensuring that the system you eventually get is both flexible and tailored to the HR needs of the business.

It is also important here that the opportunity is taken to use the introduction of 'flexibilising technology' to review and improve current HR practice. As areas prepare for major changes, asking some 'dumb' questions like 'Why do we do it this way?' or 'What is the objective of this activity?' will often pay large dividends. Without this temporary step backwards the organisation runs the risk of becoming very efficient and even very flexible in the delivery of inappropriate or even wrong outcomes.

The aim of this chapter is to introduce and evaluate the options available for flexibility from a technological perspective. By the end of the chapter you should be able to answer the following questions:

- What sort of technology will be required to support the flexibility I need?

- What are the chief benefits and possible pitfalls associated with the major technologies required for flexible working?

- How can I prepare the organisational infrastructure for flexible working?

- What can I learn from the experience of call centres in using flexible working technologies?

ASPECTS OF FLEXIBLE WORKING WHERE TECHNOLOGY CAN HELP

The best way to illustrate this is via a real situation. The case of Baxter International was reported in the journal *Flexible Working* (2000).

Teleworking at Baxter International

Baxter International is a leading US manufacturer and supplier of technology relating to the blood and circulatory systems, employing over 40,000 staff worldwide. In the late 1990s, as part of its close technological relationship with Nortel Networks, it implemented Nortel's 'HomeOffice 2' system, which connects remote workers to the corporate phone system and intranet as if they were still in the office. This system matched the need for increased flexibility for several reasons.

- The global and distributed nature of the business meant staff had to go to the office regularly in the early hours for audio conferences.

- Many of Baxter's offices, including its UK base at Compton in Berkshire, were in rural settings, and some staff had to drive substantial distances to get to and from work.

- The life-critical nature of the business meant that some staff need to available all hours to the hospitals, and to be able to direct the action required through the organisation's system. This had previously meant 24-hour rotas in the workplace, which was unpopular.

- Similarly, call centre staff at the subsidiary supplying dialysis equipment covered the period from 08:00 to 22:00, with every patient having a named agent. Working early and late was again not very popular.

Introduced in 1999, the scheme has become so popular that around 20 per cent of non-manufacturing staff now work from home, working out with their manager how often and when they come into the office. World-wide, over 3,500 employees use the teleworking system.

The set-up cost per employee was around £3,000, including the Nortel system installation, a fax, copier, printer and scanner, a desk and ergonomic chair, fire extinguisher and a smoke detector. There are also ongoing costs as the company paid for ISDN costs and personal calls. Most employees concerned had already been issued with laptops.

The organisation has gradually changed its culture in response to its distributed system of operation. Performance management is now almost totally related to outputs. Managers with home workers have needed to be trained in target-setting, measurement and relationships with their staff, for example.

A number of additional benefits have arisen since the scheme began. Retention of existing employees has improved but so has the ability to trawl through a relatively small pool of crucial specialists who no longer necessarily have to relocate to the company's main centres. This ability to avoid family disruption can be crucial in the decision whether to accept a job opportunity, as well as saving a large amount of relocation costs.

In addition, the proportion of staff returning from maternity leave has risen, as many have joined the teleworking loop and take part in audio-conferencing to keep themselves up to date.

Overall, the scheme has been seen as very successful indeed, not just for the speed of take-up by staff but by the hard-nosed measures of increases in productivity – estimated at around 30 per cent on average. Alongside this has been the substantial saving in office space.

TECHNOLOGICAL SUPPORT FOR FLEXIBLE WORKING

Volumes could be (and have been) written on the subject of technological support for flexible working. A quick inspection of the hardware and software devices available at any flexible working or IT-related conference should confirm to you that there are many solution providers willing to sell the latest flexible-working 'magic bullet'. We have looked at many of them (and from a position of some understanding), and unfortunately our view is that this magic bullet is still not available. As a result this chapter will focus on providing a sound understanding of what needs to be achieved, the options in different situations and what strategy is best suited to achieving goals for flexible working. Having read it you should be in a better position to deal with the software vendors who will find you eventually.

It is worth mentioning here that most companies are not now starting from scratch in terms of their technological architecture. HR professionals need to check what is already available in their IT area before recommending additional capability, as managers will not be thrilled with proposals for a new system that is incompatible with organisation plans and its established IT framework. At the same time it has to be said that for the great majority of organisations, investments in IT have not yielded the benefits they promised. Flexible working goes hand in hand with maximising the return on such investments, so there might just be a win–win situation here.

Where accurate repetition of processes or activities is concerned, technological automation is often the appropriate response. In this way the opposite of flexibility – rigid consistency – is what is required and delivered. Where flexible working is the goal, the need often focuses more on allowing employee mobility and enabling tasks to be done at varying times, by sharing a common knowledge and communication platform with all the relevant teams. This is where collaborative working tools such as shared access databases, electronic noticeboards, and virtual discussion groups can really help.

Unusual sources of help to working flexibly can also be found by thinking more radically or laterally. What many flexible workers need is quite simple at a basic level. They need a comfortable place to work where they have access to technology that allows quick and reliable connections to the tools and processes that enable them to do their job. One example where both of these needs are satisfied is some commercial coffee houses or cafes. We came across offerings from a range of companies who have obviously spotted this niche and are hoping to tap into the recent growth in mobile, flexible working.

In Starbucks for example, customers are now encouraged to 'Go wireless' in conjunction with T-Mobile's 'Hotspot'. The offer was intended to encourage people to use the coffee shop as a temporary place to log to web-based resources using wireless technology, so they can work remotely. Customers do have to bring their own laptops!

Using this technology for an hourly fee, you can surf the net, check e-mails and download files literally on the move – oh, and have a coffee too. Other companies have similar offerings, the largest network in the UK being BT Openzone. It has locations for a 'wire-free log on' at many railway stations, motorway service areas, hotels, cafés and fast-food restaurants.

One typical goal of flexible working is that workers who are not co-located or who rarely even meet can still operate effectively as a virtual team. The key principle is that to complete the work, all workers must have equal, unfettered access to the same data, regardless of their location or the degree of flexibility they enjoy. If this principle is breached, the flexible or remote worker quickly becomes a 'second-class' employee.

COMMUNICATIONS NETWORKS WITHIN AND OUTSIDE ORGANISATIONS

In most organisations there exist at the moment two distinct communication networks, although most experts feel that they will slowly merge as the process of digitisation increases.

The first of these is the voice infrastructure. The telephone network, although less glamorous than IT and often taken for granted, has been progressively upgrading corporate communications for many years. With the advent of smart telephones and systems features, the voice network can now support flexible working with virtual numbers that follow employees around, conference calls, call distribution (as in call centres), group pick-up, and secure, remotely accessed voicemail.

With the rise in usage of mobile telephones (there were over 35 million subscribers in the UK in 2003), capable of sending and receiving text messages (SMS) or handling wireless (WAP) communications, the voice network is going to play an increasing role in developing flexibility.

The second communications network is the one most people refer to as the IT infrastructure. The standard approach taken in most organisations is to have:

- desktop PCs for running personal applications like e-mail and Microsoft Windows programs

- servers that provide applications such as filing, databases, webwork and printing

- local area networks (LANs) connecting local PCs, servers and printers

- wide area networks (WANs) connecting sites together and connecting to the Internet.

Flexibility is greatly enhanced by the introduction of notebook PCs, and increasingly powerful personal digital assistants (PDAs) which can now do more than basic functions, and either tap into existing networks or work independently.

It is important to be clear about the advantages, features and possible problems with the range of IT networks currently in use in many organisations. Table 3 outlines the main ones.

DON'T BE FOOLED BY THE NET!

A quick search on the World Wide Web for services in pretty much any area will yield hundreds of people claiming to be experts. The offerings may be bona fide, but just as easily they could be frauds. A wonderful example of one such case is reported by Lewis (2001). He found a fantastic net-based offering which promised free expert legal advice from a resident of Perris, half-way between Palm Springs and Los Angeles. In the summer of 2000 Marcus Arnold, the son of immigrant parents from Belize, had become an expert at using a web service called AskMe.com. Anyone who accessed the AskMe.com.site could ask a question or pose a problem in any field in the hope that somebody else who was tuned in could offer an 'expert' answer.

The 'AskMe.com' site is a simple knowledge exchange. It works on the principle that anyone can use it for free, and experts in law, finance, education and the like who do not normally work for free are sometimes drawn to it as a marketing tool for their fee-charging services. Every time they answer a question the questioner can rate them, and the higher their rating goes, the more they should be able to win full fee-earning business by advertising their rating.

Marcus, who was only 15 at the time, discovered the service when he was revising for a biology exam and asked the service a question. He noticed somebody had posted up a question about a legal issue to which he knew the answer. Then came another, so he thought, why don't I answer them? He did so, using the alias LawGuy 1975. Because Marcus had the time to devote to answering more and more questions, his rating soared, as the ratings were determined by the speed of response and quality of the answer as decided by the recipient.

By 1 July Marcus was rated number 10 out of a legal expert pool of 150, many of whom were actual lawyers. Encouraged by his progress, he updated his website to make it even more attractive, and changed his pseudonym to Justin Anthony Wyrick, Jr., which he thought sounded more 'lawyerly'. This attracted more and more people seeking answers to legal

Table 3 | **Comparisons of different communications networks**

Information network type	Advantages	Features	Possible problems
Local area networks	Allows access to the same data simultaneously. Keeps security issues to a minimum.	Uses network operating systems, typically Windows NT or Netware. Standard internet protocols to provide the underlying skeleton for an intranet if one is required.	The LAN is restricted to one location, eg a building or campus. When the location is closed the LAN is inaccessible.
Intranet	Allows access to data only to those within the company 'firewall'. Facilitates good communication between staff.	Extremely flexible ways of producing things such as employee directories, groupware and databases.	Intranets are vulnerable to attack by hackers. So they need a firewall.
Extranet	A network that allows access to people outside the company such as customers, suppliers or researchers.	Generally it is a modification of an existing intranet giving access to specified groups	Security is the biggest problem, best countered by firewalls, digital signatures and message level encryption.
Internet	The breadth of coverage is unbelievably wide. All topics you can think of will be covered. Gives access to e-mail and the World Wide Web.	Search engines can be used to find the information you need. Research data and knowledge is more accessible than ever before. Distance (location) is no longer a barrier to obtaining information.	The amount of information available is so high that searches often yield too many results to deal with. Also what you see is not always what you get! (See page **102**)

problems, and as he always replied promptly, he reached number three in the ratings by the end of July.

This was all on the back of precisely no formal legal training, no studying and no accreditation or licensing by any legal association. Marcus claimed his knowledge of the law had been gleaned from hours of watching legal programmes and reality cop shows on television. He also used his net savvy to cruise the handful of legal websites that anyone could view.

The game looked like it was about to close as Marcus started being asked for his telephone number and his fee structure. Feeling a little uncomfortable, since he had never intended to deliberately deceive people, he came clean and amended his website from saying 'legal expert' to say that he was a '15-year-old intern attorney expert'.

Straight after he posted this confession, the electronic fur began to fly. Lawyers who had previously been his competitors found it easy to snare him by asking detailed legal questions he was not able to answer, and his ratings soon plummeted. This might have been the end if Marcus had not found support from 'clients' who were still happy with the advice he gave. Some people seemed to think that any 15-year-old kid who had risen so high in the ranks might just be a genius, and if he was, they wanted him on their side. With the increased publicity from his case he was able to return in the rankings, and he actually hit number one just two weeks after his announcement.

This case illustrates two principles that now have to be considered. The first is that the gap between expertise and lay knowledge is closing fast, as the Internet has made information (although arguably not true, experience-based knowledge) freely available. The second is that that net personas do not have to be true or real. The Internet is a cyberspace equivalent of the 'Wild West': anyone can set up a highly credible web presence quickly and cheaply.

PURCHASING THE KIT: PITFALLS TO AVOID

Many organisations and managers find choosing the right technological support systems tough. As a result there is often a long delay in selecting one, and this leads to frustration on the part of the staff who want to work flexibly. Those who get involved in the decision-making process but are not technological whizzes can easily be bamboozled by the language used. There is a real danger for the IT unwary of buying the wrong or out-of-date equipment. This problem can be avoided, at least in part, by following some of the steps reported here (Denbigh 2003).

1 Accept that you are not going to get it 100 per cent right. You will make mistakes, and you need to choose a vendor that will help you over the long term, not just sell and run.

2 Anticipate future requirements, not just the 'here and now'. This means talking both to internal people who know where the company is likely to be in three years' time, and to suppliers who know what is going to be on offer in three years' time. We suggest a three-year timeframe because the speed of technological change means it is difficult to predict what will be available beyond that time. Any guesses are unlikely to help you make a decision for today.

3 Assume that the hidden costs of specifying, researching, testing, customising and installing will be at least as great as the purchase costs of the kit. Talk to people who have already got the sort of system you are considering.

4 Always plan back-ups into the specifications. One of the impacts of the rise in terrorist threats over the last few years has been a reconsideration of what 'safe back-up' means. Generally speaking, if a back-up copy of data is in the same building as the original data, it is not really safe. A number of large companies have devised complete recovery plans which involve bringing new sites online within hours. Hopefully this will never be necessary, but the days when putting everything on a backup server on the next floor are over.

5 Get to work on a realistic and comprehensive policy on PC use that will prohibit the loading of games and 'private software' onto company machines – particularly 'free' downloaded programmes from the Internet, which are prone to viruses, cause system crashes, corrupt data, and load up the memory. The policy will also need to enforce certain e-mail behaviour, such as requiring users to delete any message whose sender they do not recognise without opening it. Try to think of all the things people could do with their PC that you would not want them to (there's a good brainstorm topic if ever there was one), and construct a method to prevent it.

6 Get a utilities programme like Norton Utilities, which is helpful for tidying up after the system crashes and for moving programmes around.

7 Check out the local computer support market. No telephone support line is as good as having someone turning up to fix the problem, charging by the hour.

ULTIMATE FLEXIBLE WORKING: REMOVING BARRIERS TO PERFORMANCE

The ultimate goal for increasing both flexibility and efficiency, in one of the organisations for which we have consulted recently, included the development of 'job role portals'. The idea is that whenever and wherever an employee signs in, he or she can instantly be recognised from a password, and presented with all the work tools (relevant databases, software programmes, help guides and so on) required for anyone performing that specific role. At the same time the employee can see handover notes or case files from the previous or coworkers. Daily updates on priorities and work schedules can also populate the tailored job role portal.

In this way flexibility and independence are greatly enhanced, as workers do not have to come to the information they need to do their job: it comes to them. This may well be some distance from where many organisations are at the moment, but our view is that something along these lines should not be too far away from your thoughts.

The demand for 'wi-fi networking', which uses wireless communications, has exploded over the last 12 months, according to a report in *The Times* (29 January 2004). This technology uses wi-fi boxes that transmit and receive broadband signals which can be picked up in a zone called a 'hotspot', extending around 10 metres from the box. A PDA or laptop in that zone, for example, can access the signal without being wired into the network. Some experts believe that in the near future there will be so many hotspots that users will be able to log on anywhere they wish, and be billed for access by the minute or hour. The appeal is particularly strong in older office buildings, where the cabling (if any) is insufficient for traditional communication networks. This type of networking also scores when it comes to adding in new workers, as they can also be added to the network easily without removing floorboards or ceilings to install new cables.

As an example of the ultimate in mobile working, the UK train company GNER is introducing wi-fi technology to its trains so that its customers can be connected while they are on the move.

ASPECTS OF FLEXIBLE WORKING WHERE TECHNOLOGY CANNOT HELP

The Times reported in 2004 (April 1) on a survey of 500 small firms conducted by NOP and commissioned by Microsoft, which indicated that small firms were finding it difficult to implement many of the practical aspects of flexible working. According to the report, over a third of small employers were choosing to ignore the legal requirement to allow flexible working, as the cost of non-compliance through possible tribunal awards was less than the perceived the cost of granting employees permission to work flexibly.

According to the survey, a year after the introduction of legislation to allow employees to request flexible working arrangements, fewer than 5 per cent of companies had altered their working policies to facilitate these requests. The major reason quoted for the resistance was the need to keep employees in the workplace, and keep control over what they were doing. Case study 15 illustrates a typical scenario.

The Bartons case highlights a situation where flexible working at the individual employee level cannot be made possible through technology. It is an example of a business where production is focused in one site, with a small tightly controlled team that is required to hit demanding targets. In such a situation the only way to think about flexibility is at the more macro level: that is, to

---

Case study 15: Flexible working would leave Bartons in a pickle

Bartons is a small pickle manufacturer based in St. Helens, Merseyside. It has a turnover of £1 million per year from selling pickles, sauces and chutneys to large supermarket chains. Its employees have a regular routine. They all start at 8:00 and finish at 17:00. While the company caters for emergency or unexpected absences, the tight production schedules it employs mean that everyone needs to be in place at set times. Allowing people to do things differently is not seen as an option, as the production line cannot easily be 'flexed' to allow for non-standard attendance.

Replacing absent staff from a temporary pool has a knock-on effect in that labour costs go up, damaging profitability. Holiday rotas are scheduled months in advance to ensure that the line does not falter. Joanna Fairhurst, the company general manager, admits that flexible working is a good thing for office-based jobs but sees little chance of being able to exploit it in her core business. She believes that it is the nature of the job that allows flexibility measures to work, and small-scale manufacturing generally requires employees to be on the premises, carrying out the operations of the production team. After all, her workers cannot take the bottling and packaging equipment home with them, like an office worker's laptop.

---

consider variable shift patterns, multiple locations and possibly even splitting the processes into a more modular format so that flexibility can be built in. There remains the opportunity to exploit flexibility in the non-production areas such as administration, sales, marketing and finance.

Many accepted practices that support employee effectiveness apply equally to those working flexibly. Flexible workers still need to have clear goals, appropriate resources and adequate supervision. Flexible working might indeed require more management effort to be put into supervision, to ensure that those working flexibly are well coordinated and do not waste effort on out-of-date or conflicting priorities. Technology cannot be used as a substitute for inadequate quality of communication and coordination, which is sometimes an issue to be dealt with alongside the move to flexible working.

From the HR manager's perspective, if those working flexibly are going to be operating in a very different manner from the norm, it will be worthwhile asking some preliminary questions about those areas preparing for flexible working:

- How, where and by whom will the flexible workers be supported?
- How are those working flexibly to be monitored and appraised, if they need to be?
- How will administrative issues like expenses be dealt with?
- What are the insurance, security, health and safety considerations?
- Have the legal issues such as equal opportunities, discrimination and data protection been considered and covered?

There may be technological aspects to all the items in this list, but we are talking primarily about ensuring that sound management, monitoring and control systems are in place to take account of the needs of flexible workers. Many companies just bolt on flexible working to existing policies for the sake of ease, and this may be adequate, but for many situations it is not.

Taking each of these questions in turn, Table 4 provides a good practice summary with some suggestions and issues to be considered.

DEVELOPING THE TECHNOLOGY INFRASTRUCTURE TO SUPPORT REMOTE OR MOBILE FLEXIBLE WORKING

If straightforward remote working is required, the most logical approach is to investigate how the office desktop and other services can effectively be 'stretched' to the new location. In practice this means having a company

Table 4 | **Preparing for flexible working: a guide to good practice**

Question to be asked	Good practice	Issues to consider	Suggestions
How, where and by whom will flexible workers be supported?	A 24/7 IT support team with the ability to be 'off- site'.	Costs, peak and trough support, back-up systems,	Double-loop problem solving to ensure repeated errors are not encountered.
How are those working flexibly to be monitored and appraised?	Clear, running indicators of good/poor performance with a review process.	Balance of control over empowerment. How to deal with underperformance?	Revise selection criteria for staff moving into flexible working.
How will administrative issues like expenses be dealt with?	Online HR admin services accessible remotely via intranet.	Integration with/extension of existing systems.	Use the creation of any new ways of dealing with remote HR transactions to clean up existing systems.
What are the insurance, security, health and safety considerations?	Audit assessment needed in all areas prior to launching each location.	Can existing insurances be modified? What is the plan where audit highlights deficiencies?	This set of questions need to be tackled first as they could be 'dealbreakers' for the move to flexibility.
Have the legal issues such as equal opportunities, discrimination and data protection been considered and covered?	Good practice guide should be prepared by the flexible working project manager for managers/ employees to ensure first awareness and then compliance.	Flexible workers are often inadvertently discriminated against for promotion. Who holds liability for ensuring data security?	Consultation with legal experts is a must to cover the potential downsides. Search out examples of similar operations and try to collaborate or set up joint working groups.

telephone line installed, and the computer terminal hooked up via a dedicated line to the relevant corporate network. A cheaper option is to use diverting technology to reroute incoming calls to the new location using the corporate PBX. Connecting into the company from the new location can be achieved by a modem using a form of secure hook-up to corporate intranet spaces.

While this sounds perfectly good there are drawbacks often experienced with external connections to corporate facilities. The first of these often relates to providing support, as any problems relating to connectivity are generally made more difficult by the user being off-site. Flexible users might well be operating outside the normal support shift hours, and they may have to return to the nearest support centre if they experience technical problems. In addition the speed of the connection is often too slow unless investment is made in broadband technology. The final problem area is security. Increasing concerns over breaches of secure systems mean that the remote or location-independent worker often has more security hurdles (firewalls) to pass through than conventional workers, even if the work he or she is doing is not sensitive.

Moving from a single remote location to total location independence is a major step towards total flexibility, and requires each employee to be set up as a free agent. In truth no flexible worker will ever be totally location-independent as he or she will still need to 'log on' to corporate resources. The concept should really be rebranded as 'location-variable' or mobile working.

Virtual offices have long been positioned as the way of the future, allowing workers to set up anywhere and dispense with the concept of main and branch offices. The closer we get to the paperless office, the more this concept will be applicable. The technology infrastructure for a location-variable worker has to adhere to the following principles;

- web-enabled location of all corporate IT applications on a dedicated secure server available from a totally reliable business Internet service provider (with a back-up strategy for when reliability fails)

- fast and safe Internet access for all

- wherever possible paper systems replaced by electronic delivery

- full exploitation of groupware and intranets to facilitate shared knowledge; discussion groups and messaging; online manuals, directories and catalogues for relatively static material

- access to stored documents and presentations

- electronic administration of activities such as holidays and expenses

- shared filing systems

- Internet access portal for approved or preferred sites.

A more adventurous option is to employ the services of a third-party organisation to service the remote working capability of the organisation. This involves sourcing support and technological resources from an outside company to take over all aspects of home or remote-working support. In this way the direct costs of facilitation of remote flexible working can at least be quantified, and compared with the benefits gained through savings on office space or productivity gains.

A FLEXIBLE HALF-WAY HOUSE OR THE NEW FACTORIES? THE RISE OF CALL CENTRES

Call centres have been a major development in the working environment over the last decade. *The Teleworking Handbook* by Alan Denbigh (2003) claims that there are now over 5,000 call centres in the UK alone.

Call centres can exhibit a range of the features of flexible working depending upon the perspective from which they are considered. The location of the call centre is often the first manifestation of flexibility, as many of them have been located away from the original business setting in places where labour is available and fixed costs are lower. The high labour turnover rates experienced (typically 30–40 per cent each year) operate against these savings, at least to a degree.

Inside the call centre, many of the features of flexible working we have been discussing (such as key time working, variable hours and flexible shift patterns) are typically found. In addition, depending on the type of call centre, the work itself can be sourced from various locations. The screen-based system typically prompts the operator to use a range of preset greetings depending on the client's requirements. In this way organisations that do not have sufficient need or resources for an independent call centre can benefit by plugging into an existing service as and when they need it.

Sometimes referred to as the modern equivalent of the industrial revolution's 'dark satanic mills', many call centres are not dark and do not look very menacing, but they are often taken to represent the popular face of flexible working. As such there are a range of issues that need to be addressed by the HR manager to ensure the maximum benefit is gained from their introduction.

What is a call centre?

In call centres, workers sit at computer terminals and make or answer telephone calls about their employer's (or its client's) business. They can be small or massive in size. They can be found in the public, private and privatised sectors. Staff work their way through computer programs to answer the caller's questions, take orders, record details and so on.

One of the biggest problems reported by call centre workers is the pace of work. Many require workers to meet targeted numbers of calls. Centres often have a screen showing the rate of calls being processed, and the technology that underpins the calls can now be used to monitor activity rates very closely. A forced pace of work may improve productivity over short timespans but it can also lead to stress, repetitive strain injuries and other forms of ill-health.

The employer's statutory requirement to provide a 'safe system of work' applies as much to call centres as anywhere else. If the repetitive and monotonous nature of the work leads people to complain of 'repetitive brain injury' or 'zombiefication', any productivity gains are likely to be short-lived and can even be outweighed by higher absenteeism and labour turnover.

Some of the more common complaints that can affect call centre workers more than their counterparts in traditional offices include:

- *Voice loss.* Call centre workers' voices are under great pressure because of the nature of their work. Conditions affecting the voice (dysphonia) can be short or long-term, and some are permanent.

- *Stress.* Call centre staff are likely to have to endure customer complaints about failures in service, poor-quality goods, delivery of the wrong goods and so on. Clients can become very agitated when things go wrong, and dealing with this constantly can be a stressor for the worker.

- *Sight disorders.* Computer operators have reported such symptoms as soreness or dryness of the eyes, blurred vision, light sensitivity and headaches from working long hours in front of a VDU screen. This is referred to as computer vision syndrome. It requires the employer to provide regular eye tests, frequent breaks away from the screen, additional lighting where needed and other precautions.

- *Rest and toilet breaks.* In a highly pressured environment and where workers have to sit in one position all day at work, sometimes for many hours, they need breaks away from their workstation. Natural breaks like going to the toilet, refreshment or lunch breaks help, but may not be enough.

In order to help overcome these and other issues with call centre working, the Call Centre Association (CCA) has developed a code of best practice for all its members This code is divided into five sections, and covers:

- people issues
- communications within the call centre
- culture
- policies and legislation
- performance and efficiency.

Under the section on people issues, the code ensures that employees at all levels are given mandatory training and development to support them in their role, which is evaluated for its design to achieve their own and the organisation's objectives. As is generally accepted elsewhere, the CCA code insists that a performance development process be in place, and employee personal development plans are the norm. In addition the code requires that individual employees are aware of their personal and/or team objectives and organisational goals, together with the means by which they are monitored.

In terms of communication internal to the call centre, the code asks for processes to be in place to gather employees' views, disseminate information and take appropriate action. A documented process must also be available to resolve inter-employee and employee–management disputes.

With regard to the culture of the call centre, the code insists that all recruitment policies be legally compliant and that there be a commitment on the employer side to provide an honest forecast of potential for progression or development. And to address commonly found turnover problems, measures are to be set for attrition and attendance, with plans in place to achieve or maintain standards.

The code makes a point of highlighting the fast pace of movement in legislation surrounding call centre working, and recommends that a process is in place to ensure that developing legislative requirements are brought to the attention of management. Beyond this, managers and supervisors are to be trained in the application of current legislation and are mandated to apply it.

The final section of the code covers issues of call centre performance. As might be expected this is the most lengthy section, as the whole *raison d'être* for many call centres is to be quicker or more effective than alternatives in providing service delivery.

The code focuses on where standards are to be set and measured for key activities. These standards are to be understood by employees, and plans must be in place to achieve and/or maintain them. In addition customer complaints should be logged and reviewed so that action can be taken to eliminate recurring complaints.

A process needs to be in place to gather customer feedback, to ensure that the call centre is operating effectively and not just efficiently. Targets need to be set for customer satisfaction, and plans need to be in place to achieve or maintain them

Given that the call centre will typically be located remotely arrangements need to be in place to manage call centre internal relationships with other business areas and to identify, review and resolve issues as they arise. In particular contingency and resiliency plans are in place, are kept up to date and are practised.

If all the conditions of the CCA code of best practice were met, it could be argued that far from being 'modern day sweatshops', well-run call centres represent a vast improvement on the way that more traditional organisations manage their activities.

MONITORING FLEXIBLE WORK AND FLEXIBLE WORKERS

The aims of monitoring flexible working are the same as for any other type of working: to establish whether the benefits are being maximised. The starting point for any monitoring process must be a form of quantification of the benefits, in order that comparisons can be made against non-flexible or traditional working.

One option is to track improvements as a result of flexible working in areas such as service delivery. Typical straightforward measures include:

- reductions in 'downtime' for customer services or operations departments: using flexible working and shift patterns it is possible to cover unsocial hours, or transfer work to different time zones

- reductions in lost calls or failed calls in call centre operations by transferring peak workloads to alternative sites or contingent employees

- time spent with customers by mobile staff, as opposed to 'wasted' time spent travelling

- improved response times for situations where customers require on-site attention.

Claims for increases in productivity by flexible operating can sometimes sound outlandish, but if for example an employee is able to carry out four customer visits per day in place of three, that is an improvement of 33 per cent. Of course this may not be translated into an increase in sales or revenue, but the potential is clear.

A range of indirect or additional measures might prove useful in monitoring the effects of flexible working. These can be divided into two broad categories. The first concern the typically one-off changes in physical assets and structural change that result from the introduction of flexibility, and the second involve improvements in the effectiveness of human assets. In the first category savings can typically be realised by using less office space or even sharing desk or administrative support facilities, where previously all staff had their own space and demanded their own support. The HR function should be ideally positioned to gather data on the second, more ongoing category to see if any changes in unauthorised absence, labour turnover figures, or staff motivation, stress levels and morale could be attributable to the use of flexible working.

It is also possible to monitor the progress of flexible working by undertaking reviews at key milestones. By establishing stakeholder focus groups it should be possible to determine if the expected benefits of flexible working are materialising, and if any areas are not working well, the possibility for early intervention is secured.

One of the chief concerns that many managers have over flexible working is a result of not being able to see and directly supervise staff: a loss in the confidence that people working when they are supposed to be, and are doing the right things when at work. In a traditional office environment managers often naively feel they can identify the hard workers by observation. However, the phenomenon of 'presentism' has been reported as a common response by employees, who have recognised that being in the office early and staying late is all that matters, regardless of the level of productivity or quality of the work they do. Interestingly the UK has the record for the longest working hours in Europe, especially amongst managers and professional staff, yet output is no more efficient than it is in countries where shorter working hours are the norm. This should tell UK managers something: it is not the time taken that really counts, but the outputs achieved. Flexible working is an ideal opportunity to move towards monitoring by outputs not inputs, which is what many OD specialists have been preaching for a number of years, when it comes to the effective monitoring of knowledge workers.

The managerial control of employees working entirely from home challenges many of the accepted practices of traditional management. Monitoring and control activities that involve management observation or recording of employee presence, for example via a time clock, need to be adapted significantly for use in home-based employment. Felstead, Jewson and Walters (2003) reported findings in this area from a study of over 200 interviews with managers and employers in 13 different organisations. They investigated the control of home-working employees by asking what challenges were presented to traditional mechanisms that rely on visibility and employee presence. They also sought to capture the techniques and adaptations being made on the part of managers to get over such challenges.

The findings they present show that five groupings of techniques were being implemented by managers in organisations seeking to reassure themselves that home workers were productive. These were classified as:

- new surveillance devices

- activating existing managerial surveillance devices

- setting short and medium output targets, regularly monitored

- bringing management into the home environment

- emphasising trust.

If the use of new, sophisticated surveillance devices involves significant cost, it would appear to defeat one of the key objectives of introducing home working, which is often reducing expenses. Consequently the most common forms of new surveillance were found to be relatively inexpensive open diaries (electronic or otherwise), so anyone could see what activities the home workers were recording. The use of regular telephone update calls by managers, and home visits to check on progress, were also reported as relatively effective monitoring techniques. These techniques were seen as key to allowing the manager to gather a sense of employee well-being or attitude, which would normally be picked up quite easily in an office environment, but was now hidden through the lack of visibility.

Some home workers were not happy about managers visiting them at home, as they felt it was an unwarranted intrusion on personal space. As a consequence the degree of trust between the manager and the home worker has to be high. For some companies a qualification period is normal before permission to work from home is granted. In this way the company can be sure it is getting a good return from the home worker for its investment in technology and training. For other companies this trust was manifested in the employees' ability to be self-motivated and self-disciplined.

CONCLUSION

In this chapter we have showed how and where the application of modern technology can support and enhance flexible working. We have also outlined some of the possible pitfalls, and situations where technology alone will not solve the problems of flexibility. It is inevitable that by the time you read this book, further advances in technology will have been made and people will be moving to flexibilise jobs or services that were not previously thought of as candidates for such ways of working.

4
Making flexibility work in practice

TAKING A STRATEGIC VIEWPOINT

All too often, flexible working is seen as distinct process or a limited initiative that takes place within a certain sector or layer of the organisation. It is seen as tactical rather than strategic, reactive rather than proactive. Although a minority of organisations have introduced flexibility strategically as a deliberate, planned step towards the goal of increased competitiveness or improved service provision, far too many have simply capitalised on the short-term opportunities derived from flexible working as a convenient answer to today's challenging issue. Rarely do you see a full joined-up jigsaw of practices that match the organisation's culture and service its business imperatives.

It can be argued that successful implementation needs an effective culture-change programme, one that has relatively distinct goals in terms of values and beliefs, processes and behaviours (Knell and Savage 2001). This can apply especially to larger organisations where long-term strategic thinking has a strong influence. It sounds complicated, but many organisations have a great deal of the tools and equipment in place. When mission statements and sets of guiding values are examined, most include the need for flexibility and the encouragement to enhance skills. These simply need to be translated into an integrated approach, linking the specific employer-driven initiatives set out in Chapter 2 (annualised hours, multi-skilling and so on) with the employee and legislation-driven requirements set out in Chapter 1.

Some organisations have linked them through the balancing process. 'We want you to buy in to the employer initiatives and all the changes to working practices we need, because they make us work much more efficiently and productively. in return, we will help you to achieve a work–life balance with the aid of family-friendly and leisure-friendly benefits.' This new form of psychological contract has been extended further through the attempt to become 'an employer of choice', as shown in the Lloyds TSB case study (16).

Case study 16: Lloyds TSB Work Options scheme

A series of mergers in the 1990s provided Lloyds TSB (incorporating Cheltenham and Gloucester Building Society and Scottish Widows) with the opportunity to question its methods of competing for staff. The end of the 'jobs for life' culture in the early 1990s meant that to keep good staff, Lloyds TSB had to differentiate itself as an employer not just from other banks but from the wider retail sector. There were also equal opportunity challenges, since 66 per cent of the workforce was female but only 11 per cent of senior management. Existing flexible working arrangements were ad hoc and small-scale local initiatives reacting to local needs. Recent staff surveys had also pointed to the lack of flexibility as a reason for staff turnover and poor perceptions of the organisation.

In 1998, the board approved a strategy to create an integrated and open flexible working initiative run by a centralised project group, overseen by a steering group of directors from across the group boards. The philosophy was set out by five guiding principles:

- Meeting business goals will remain our priority.

- Equity means equal access to a fair process.

- Working in partnership (managers and staff).

- Job performance is relevant.

- Flexibility is not an entitlement.

Although somewhat forbidding and almost restricting, these principles were necessary to ensure senior management gave full backing to the initiative, an essential requirement to ensure progress was swift and supportive. Backing was also given by trade unions, and staff focus groups approved the philosophy. The purely voluntary nature of the arrangement and the non-contractual aspect encouraged managers to work out with their teams and individual employees how they could provide a better service to customers, meet the business's changing needs and respond to the particular, personal requirements of all staff.

The scheme proved extremely successful in its early years, and the CEO, Peter Elwood, reported in 2002 that the Work Options scheme had 'together with our excellent range of other benefits, really given us the edge over our competitors'.

Sources: Wustemann (1999), Rana (2002).

For Microsoft, the company that nearly always tops the polls for employer of choice, flexibility is a key part of its employment culture strategy, for which it has won numerous awards. This was explained by Steve Harvey, UK director of people and culture as:

> *We want people to understand that it's their choice to be working at Microsoft. It was my choice that I played golf yesterday – I hadn't played for weeks, fancied a game and wanted to catch up with a business contact. I'm empowered to do that if I want do. Everybody knows my diary is open and if I choose to work Sunday nights, I can play golf on Monday morning. I'm no different to thousands of other employees. That's what it's about.*

> *(Persaud 2003)*

Not every manager is easily convinced by good-sounding ideas, and sometimes they can only be signed off by the board after research has been carried out. BT, for example, wanted to be sure that its teleworkers would be as productive as those with conventional working conditions. It began to investigate this in 1998 by identifying a pilot site (its Cardiff Engineering centre) and establishing baseline measures for productivity, turnover and employee engagement.

Next, it designed a series of interventions introducing flexible working, and observed the three variables at intervals over the next three years, as well as carrying out tests to ensure that flexibility had an effect on productivity. At the end of the period, it found there had been a significant increase in productivity, a substantial reduction in turnover and a notable increase in employee engagement (Gratton 2003).

Without that essential strategic driving force, it is much harder for policies and initiatives to fall on fertile ground and bring a productive harvest.

WORKING OUT A POLICY

Once the general strategy and direction have been decided, policy decisions need to be made on the nature of the flexible working schemes. These include the following aspects.

- *Should the guidelines attempt to cover all aspects of the operations, introducing rules to cover all eventualities or should they aim for simplicity, an absence of bureaucracy and excessive rules?*

  At ASDA, 'the secret of success is simplicity,' reported Marie Gill, head of colleague relations (*PM* online 2004). 'You must proceed on the basis of trust – not in a belief that people will try to abuse the system.' All the flexible schemes introduced, such as school-starter, spring holidays for older workers (so-called Benidorm leave) and elder care leave, underpin ASDA's fundamental belief in 'respect for the individual'.

There are a number of risks with the simplicity approach, however. First, there are complications with all flexible schemes, and HR departments may be faced with a barrage of questions relating to the fine detail of, say, job-share or annualised hours. Second, without detailed guidance managers might authorise inconsistent decisions in difficult areas, such as home working or family leave. Inconsistency can lead to a sense of injustice in the organisation, and reduce the level of trust. At worst, it can lead to tribunal claims. Third, without sufficient detailed guidance, managers may decide that they will opt out of the responsibilities and not get involved, to the detriment of the needs of their staff.

So a balance has to be sought between these two viewpoints. Certainly there is a need to emphasise the principles of the schemes in the most simple way, but then sufficient guidance should be provided on the details through training and communication systems.

- *Should the organisation introduce a raft of flexible schemes as a 'big bang' approach, or use an incremental approach, with a steady stream of improvements and extensions?*

From a strategic viewpoint, a move to a more flexible, empowered and open culture matching the business needs will often be accompanied by a variety of flexible initiatives. Blackburn and Darwen Council's first initiatives, for example, accompanied its fundamental shift in managerial emphasis from the traditional concept of 'presenteeism' (assuming that someone's presence equates to productive work) to one that examined and measured the quality of employees' work and how they met the service requirements of the council. Now, following three very successful pilots in the social services department, it encourages managers and employees to work in partnership to find new and innovative ways of working (Tarpey 2004).

- *How can you prevent certain areas of flexibility from being simply 'women's issues'?*

Work–life balance has all too often been seen as a means for providing female-friendly benefits in the organisation – child care facilities, enhanced maternity leave and so on. Since the late 1990s, there has been a drive for the policies to become all-inclusive and to encourage equal take-up by men and women. The European Working Time regulations have played a large part here in trying to address the long hours culture, and there has been much greater emphasis on working all the initiatives into improving the flexible labour market with free movement of labour, balancing employee and employer needs.

When establishing the organisation's policy, therefore, it is essential to stress the importance for all employees, and consciously to market the policies to both men and women at all levels. Ernst and Young, for example, has a policy statement on work–life balance that stresses that the organisation is committed to providing staff with the flexibility required to address family, caring and other responsibilities, yet also providing a first-class customer service (Treneman 2002).

In the public sector, the policy needs can have a different slant, although the need to show bottom-line savings remains paramount. Retention of staff, reduced absenteeism, higher staff satisfaction trends and a much reduced use of agency staff linked to greater employee empowerment can be driving forces, as shown in the NHS case study number 17.

Another key consideration is the relationship of the organisation to its community. For Telford and Wrekin Borough Council, the key driver for the introduction of flexible working practices was its need to support its local community. As John Harris, head of personnel and development, indicated: 'As we are one of the largest employers in the area, with 5,500 staff, it is important that we are good employers. If we help our employers at work, it helps the community,'

The borough has one of the highest concentration of single mothers in Europe, and as roughly 80 per cent of the council's workforce is female, a range of practices has been introduced to enable mothers to return to work and generally help working parents. These include a workplace crèche, assistance with child care costs, local shop discounts and a hotline to a nursery for those needing emergency child care. Most important are working hours that allow parents to combine careers with bringing up children.

Managers are devolved responsibility to handle all individual requests, and they are expected to initiate work–life balance conversations and act as role models by looking after their own work–life balance. To ensure consistency and fairness, managers are assessed on the work–life competencies in their department through a management development programme. Workshops organised internally have been offered to other

---

Case study 17: Paediatric intensive care unit at Guy's and St Thomas's Trust

In 2002, Guy's Hospital was trying to operate its paediatric unit with a vacancy level of 44 per cent, and realised it could not go on in that way, cancelling urgent operations and providing a poor customer service. Led by the chief executive with full management support, the hospital entered into a full staff consultation through 'discovery interviews' to identify all the working environment issues. This was followed up by an extensive action plan to develop and strengthen roles (such as health care assistants having a more clinical focus) and create rotational posts which allow nurses to leave the shift system for six months to undertake development and prevent burn-out. Working hours were made more flexible, and there was a much greater effort made to devolve problem-solving to local staff.

The initiative was soon recognised as a major success. Over the first year of operation, vacancies dropped to 2 per cent, there was a substantial reduction in agency hours, and cancelled operations fell from 18 to 2. A year later, it was 'highly commended' in the NHS Management awards sponsored by the *Health Service Journal*, with the judges recognising that it was driven by a clear and decisive business case.

Source: Working Families (2003)

---

employers in the area, and a number have joined in. All this is just another service for the community.

Since introducing these practices, the council has been able to keep its offices open an extra three days a year and for longer hours. Sickness levels have dropped from 13 to 8 per cent (lower than the national average) and the council has one of the lowest staff turnovers in the UK.

Source: Woolnough (2003).

Flexible working standards and accreditation

Another approach that can be used in any sector is to adopt a flexible working *set of standards*. A number are available for work–life balance, including those produced by Investors in People, launched in 2003, and Work Life Balance Consultancy (WLBC). They provide a comprehensive checklist against which to measure the organisation's aims and performance. As with any accreditation system, the organisation works towards achieving the required standards, and when this is achieved, will receive accreditation from the appropriate licensing body, which will have provided guidance and assistance in the process.

Under the WLBC system, launched in 2001, there are groups of standards under the following headings:

- Leadership and Commitment

- Systems and Planning

- Action

- Review and Assessment.

The standards for leadership and commitment designed by WLBC are set out in Figure 2.

PRACTICAL IMPLICATIONS

This section is devoted to practical implications for the successful introduction of the flexible working systems described earlier in the book. Because each scheme is context-specific, the advice will inevitably tend to be of a general nature, but checklists are always valuable to remind potential users of essential requirements.

First, here is some generic advice that applies in all flexible working situations:

- *Involve* members of the work teams in the planning for the scheme. They are far more likely to promote a scheme which they have helped plan.

- *Monitor and evaluate.* At the time that each major milestone is reached, a review should be scheduled to evaluate the current success of the scheme measured against the planned outcomes. Improvements in areas such as productivity, quality, customer service and absenteeism must be measured and assessed to judge if the initiative is on target.

- Get *feedback* from employees on a regular basis, through the formal staff consultation channels or through an attitude survey, and be prepared to change the scheme, especially where ideas arise from the employees themselves. It is important to pick up on any major dissatisfaction at an early stage, rather than allow discontent to fester and early support for the scheme to dwindle.

Figure 2 | **Leadership and commitment**

1 You are committed to setting up work–life balance arrangements through your policies and culture.	• Senior managers can describe the reason for your work–life balance policies. • Senior managers can explain your work–life balance policies and values. • Employees can describe the benefits for them, their colleagues and the organisation resulting from the work–life balance policies and culture.
2 You have work–life balance policies and practices that form part of an overall strategy, to improve business performance.	• Senior managers describe how you meet your legal obligations in relation to work–life balance issues. • Senior managers can describe how you have considered using all five categories of work–life balance arrangements. • Senior managers can describe how you have considered using best-practice solutions to work–life balance issues. • Employees can explain why you have a work–life balance strategy. • Senior managers can describe the results they expect from the work–life balance strategy.
3 You make sure that all employees know about your work–life balance policies and systems.	• Employees can explain your work–life balance policies and systems. • You have written terms and conditions relating to work–life balance that explain what employees are entitled to and what you may offer.
4 You are committed to consulting your employees on work–life balance issues.	• The people involved in consultation can confirm that it has been effective and that it emphasises the joint responsibility of you and your employees in achieving realistic solutions. • Your consultation systems must meet legal and regulatory obligations and be told to all employees. • Employees confirm that you have asked them about work–life balance issues and are able to discuss them with their line manager or another senior manager.

- *Communicate the successes* of the scheme to the employees on a regular basis, using articles in company newsletters, intranet postings or old-fashioned noticeboards.

- *Celebrating and recognising success* is also important from an early stage. Using any of the usual recognition devices, such as a letter from the chief executive, a special (if small) one-off payment or paying for a celebratory departmental lunch, can also reinforce the success of any of the schemes, as long as it is seen as appropriate within the organisational culture.

The next section gives some summarised advice in specific areas of flexibility.

Advice on job-sharing

- Have clear policies that spell out the rights and obligations of each party to the job-share.

- Informal arrangements can only really work effectively in smaller operations and may cause confusion at a later date.

- Ensure that your policies are non-discriminatory.

- Provide guidance for managers who will have to monitor and review the performance of the job-sharing scheme.

- Clarify the performance indicators applicable to the job-share scheme such as cost savings or increased flexibility, and be clear how these will be measured.

Advice on career breaks

- Provide support for the employees once they leave to keep them in touch with developments, for example via an alumni network.

- Invite employees who are part of the scheme to regular catch-up meetings.

- Consider gradual reintroduction of the employee via part-time employment.

- Do not offer guarantees over the seniority position or place of work when the employee returns, as the level of change experienced usually makes such promises difficult to honour.

- Work to secure a tripartite understanding between the employee, his or her department or area, and HR over the precise arrangements of the break.

Advice on downshifting

- Do ensure that the experience brought by new downshifting employees is both relevant and current.

- Explore where possible the reasons behind the desire to downshift before agreeing.

- Consider the effects of having highly experienced employees placed in more junior positions on your existing managers.

Advice on introducing annualised hours/flexible hours

- Do not attempt a scheme unless your business has sufficient signs of labour utilisation slackness, such as periods of lay-off and permanent overtime, indicating a considerable saving can be made.

- Work with line managers to agree the baseline of working, especially the absolute minimum number of employees required to run a shift or service operation efficiently without sickness or any other disrupting factors.

- Do not allow line managers to include any additional factors when calculating base staffing, no matter how hard they argue their necessity.

- Consider who are the winners and losers from the scheme, and ensure that there is some appropriate compensation for losers who may be influential on obtaining the scheme's acceptance.

- Ensure that you include in the calculations opportunities for employees to benefit by working more smartly and thereby working fewer hours. Make sure that there are a number of bank hours which will not be used if the operations run smoothly.

- Be prepared for redundancies, which are usually associated with the introduction of such schemes, with a voluntary scheme prepared or robust criteria for selection if voluntary redundancies do not produce sufficient numbers.

Advice on introducing multi-skilling

Step 1: Identify key actions linked to business priorities

The starting point for any successful initiative is the clear vision of a 'big idea' which has immediate and long-term benefits to the organisation. All the benefits of multi-skilling listed earlier in this section must be specifically targeted so that a coherent plan is put together which can be easily sold. A champion is needed to draw up the plan and devise it in such a way that it can convince all the stakeholders.

It will be necessary to persuade the board of the bottom-line benefits so funds can be released to invest in the training. It will be necessary to convince management and supervision that the long-term additional effect on their part in organising and monitoring the training will be worthwhile. Finally, the employee groups themselves will have to appreciate the all-round benefits and accept any changes in their terms and conditions that may apply.

The overall plan will need to include:

- the strategic link with business requirements
- how current major problems are solved
- a cost–benefit analysis
- the resources required, including any IT development to support the initiative
- the time scale involved.

Step 2: Consult with the workforce and sell the ideas

All ideas need selling, even those that appear to have obvious benefits. The consultation programme is not just to obtain the necessary consent to fundamental changes, such as where formal union agreements are concerned, but also to change the mindsets associated with static jobs and routine activities.

In Nottingham Hospital Trust (Johnson 1999), for example, multi-skilling required fundamental changes in the organisation structure, and consultation throughout the departments involved was necessary. The outcome was a general agreement to pilot the changes in the theatre directorate area, a department where many of the staff were keen to try their hand in this initiative. This gave a much better chance of a positive outcome, and was a far better process than imposing the initiative on resentful and unconvinced employee groups. Moreover, staff in the department were given a choice of three new rostering patterns to consider, and the majority decision on one specific pattern again made the implementation of this scheme much smoother.

Similarly, at Barclaycall, extensive consultation took place through employee forums so that employees could put forward constructive ideas on how the scheme should work, and how greater job satisfaction could be achieved (IDS 2000b).

Step 3: Identify the detailed training requirement

Introducing multi-skilling provides the opportunity for a long, hard look at how jobs are carried out and the skills and knowledge that are required. Efficient job design is essential so that the training needs for each role can be analysed effectively and a lean training programme put together. This can be an expensive exercise, so any superfluous job activities should be cut out ruthlessly.

Once the roles are clarified, the skills assessment can take place. This involves identifying how many skills are required by how many staff, and matching this against their existing skill levels. Decisions will need to be made about the minimum levels of skills required for an employee to be classified as multi-skilled.

Step 4: Decide on the processes of multi-skilling

The three main decisions to be taken here are:

- Will any payment for multi-skilling be involved?
- How will trainees be chosen?
- What methods of training will be used and will accreditation apply?

Step 5: Plan the training programme, including methods and implications of release

Once the detailed decisions are made on the processes involved, the comprehensive plan can be put together, with the milestones clearly indicated for each section. It is common to start the programme with a pilot scheme and then allow time for a review so the bugs can be worked out of the system. Once the plan is fully detailed, it allows much of the activity to be delegated to line management, working closely with the HR department. Experience has shown that that most of the training will be on the job, so line managers need to be empowered to take decisions within the agreed criteria on selection, training, accreditation and payment. A simple administration and authorisation process also needs to be laid down.

It is essential that the schemes are owned locally by line managers and their staff and not seen as a centralised HR-driven system. Achievement of the milestones needs to be incorporated into the performance management targets for line management and HR.

Step 6: Monitor, evaluate and celebrate success

Using any of the standard recognition devices, such as a letter from the chief executive, a special (if small) one-off payment or paying for a celebratory departmental lunch, can also reinforce the success of the scheme, as long as it is seen as appropriate within the organisational culture.

Advice on outsourcing

Deciding whether to outsource

Some of the questions that need to put before initiating the process are:

- Are there any security points that would encourage or discourage outsourcing?

- What is the nature of the process to be outsourced? If it is a core activity, outsourcing should proceed with extreme caution even where the other factors are encouraging.

- Can performance measures easily be put in place to ensure that satisfactory progress is made by the provider?

- What are the key objectives? Is the core objective improved performance or cost saving, or a combination of the two? Can the objectives be quantified?

- Are there any viable alternatives to outsourcing, such as a joint operation or a further attempt at in-house improvement?

- What skills may be lost through the process? Will the overall training and development policy of the organisation be affected?

Setting the standards

Issues here include the more obvious areas relating to operations, which have to be clear, unambiguous but not too complex, but also areas such as the quality of the staff involved. This may be measurable in terms of qualification or experience (although many excellent IT staff can be unqualified and much experience is measured in weeks rather than years), but standards of behaviour and attitude are far more difficult to define. It is better to try to involve outsourced staff in company affairs relating to training or social activities, so they become better integrated into the company culture.

Controlling the contract

There are two parts to this. The first is ensuring that the process for agreeing a contract is carried out successfully. This involves the drawing-up of the specification, including the length of the contract and the nature of any penalties for non-performance, the way that a short list of contractors will be selected, how bids will be invited, evaluated and awarded. Under best value, this process is circumscribed by law and common practice, and needs considerable skill, experience and expertise to avoid claims from potential providers who have been excluded.

The second part in the process concerns how to manage the contract itself. There have been a number of experiences under best value where contracts have been awarded to providers who have offered the lowest tender, but the authority has been hostile to that provider for historical or personal reasons. (The authority may have wanted to keep the contract in-house.) Most of these contracts have ended in acrimony, as the authority has acted to the letter of the contract rather than its spirit and this can lead to its invoking unfair penalties. It is clear from this experience that generally, contracts will only work effectively if there is mutual understanding and a good degree of trust. There has to be allowance at the start of the contract, as the provider learns about the details of the contract and the organisation, recruits the staff and gets the work under way. There has to be a judgment over how long the 'probationary period' is – for catering, it is very short indeed as staff expect an improved service from day one – and how reasonable it is to threaten applying penalty clauses if they form part of the contract, and the nature of those penalties.

Terms and conditions of provider's employees

It is always a difficult situation if employees of two different organisations are working side by side under different terms and conditions. Back in the 1970s, unions used to insist that subcontractors coming onto employer's premises must be paid the same rates, although complex bonus arrangements often clouded this point. Today, unions rarely have powers to influence this situation, but it can still affect the morale of employees if the provider's employees have far better terms. It is worth setting up a system of careful liaison to try to avoid areas of gross comparison.

Transferring employees

Apart for the complexities of TUPE, there is the major issue of how and when to tell the staff involved. Reilly and Tamkin (1996) set out the two views:

One view is to do it as late as possible, to minimise the risk of sabotage, and only through the incoming contractor, who then has early opportunity to state their case. This means that staff hear directly from their potential future employer who can address their concerns. The alternative opinion is the diametric opposite. It argues that concerns over sabotage are exaggerated and precautions can be put in place to reduce the risk. The principal aims of the transition, it is felt, should be to gain employee support for the process and minimise fear of the unknown. This, it is believed, will be assisted by early information which avoids rumour developing.

Transferring back

An unusual situation arose when Lloyds Bank merged with TSB. An evaluation off the IT facilities at the joint operation showed that outsourced work could be brought back in-house. A five-year contract with Sema, entered into in 1996, was terminated by agreement, and the 100 staff involved were told at first that they would simply transfer back to Lloyds TSB without any compensation. However, after negotiation with the BIFU union, it was agreed that they could remain with Sema, take voluntary redundancy at enhanced rates, or transfer back with a 5 per cent pay rise and a £2,000 lump sum.

Philip Vernon, European partner and outsourcing specialist at Mercer HR Consulting, has given the following advice on getting outsourcing right (Hammond 2002):

- Be clear why you are going into outsourcing. If you are using it as a way of offloading a problem you don't want to deal with, you will run into trouble.

- Make sure you and the contractor have a common view of what you want to get out of the contract and what they are expected to deliver. That shared vision needs to be established right at the beginning.

- Check out the contractor's track record. You need to be confident that they can deliver what you need. If they have done it for someone else, they are more likely to be able to do it for you.

- Do the sums. You need to know how much it is costing you to provide the service at the moment and exactly what the service entails. In a commercial arrangement you pay for what you get. What frequently happens with outsourced contracts is the client gets a nasty shock when they are billed for things that they didn't realise they were using or being charged for.

- Ask yourself: 'Is this an organisation we can work with?' If you have a long-term agreement you are going to have to work together over a number of years, so you have to feel you can trust them.

- Manage the contract. There is a temptation to think that outsourcing means you are not responsible for it any more, but managing your supplier is as critical as any internal management. If it is a sizeable contract you may need to put a group of people on it. Closely governing the contract is the only way you will pick up on problems and be able to deal with them before they get out of hand.

Dealing with temporary employees

Choosing an interim manager provider

Neil Fogarty (2002), practice director of IMS Interim Management, gives the following advice in choosing an interim provider and managing the relationship:

- Ensure that the interim executive put forward by the provider has the sector and functional expertise, that he or she levers off his/her own practical experience as opposed to the reputation of the provider.

- Also ensure he/she has the credibility, by checking with clients he/she has previously worked for in an interim capacity.

- Access the knowledge network – the provider must actively manage its considerable network of interim executives.

- Always focus on the 'solution' that you require, rather than the technicality of the CV.

- Cultivate one provider, rather than testing the water.

- Ensure clarity and transparency throughout, including complete understanding of the required outcomes and the fees, including the provider's margins.

SAYING NO AND OTHER DIFFICULTIES

As detailed in Chapter 1, the Employment Act 2002 gives a list of grounds on which a request for flexible working may be turned down, such as the burden of extra costs, detrimental impact on productivity, quality or performance. In fact the list would seem to provide a get-out clause for each and every request.

The reality appears to be a little different. In a CIPD/Lovells research study (2003), a large number of the employers contacted said they generally had little difficulty with the new right, with 90 per cent reporting no significant problems and 76 per cent saying they had no difficulty complying with the legislation. A more recent survey (CIPD 2005) found that 66 per cent of organisations surveyed reported an increase in the number of employees making use of flexible working. In one private survey in the NHS, one unit had 10 respondents where no requests were turned down, and there were four examples where employees' requests were either refused or stopped after a trial period:

- A health visitor asked if she could reduce her hours from five to four and not work Fridays. In the area in which she worked, there was hardly any cover on a Friday, because many part-timers wanted Friday off. She was refused but it was agreed for her to have a different day off each week.

- One member of staff wanted to work flexible hours each day but she had to be limited to between 8:00 and 18:00 as no service was required outside these hours.

- Because of the effect on the equity of the other members of the team, a team member's request for reduced hours had to be turned down.

- One trial of flexible hours had to be stopped because of the timekeeping of the employee concerned.

In general, where requests have been turned down, they have been mostly on the grounds of the employer's inability to reorganise work among existing staff and the detrimental effect on the ability to meet customer demand. Tribunal claims arising from these refusals have been few and far between. This is probably because the only basis of the claim can be the employer's failure to follow the statutory procedure, or because the employer has rejected an application based on incorrect facts.

If a claim is upheld, the tribunal may require the employer to reconsider the application and/or award compensation of up to eight weeks' pay (capped at the statutory week's pay). However, it is possible that some applicants may claim that the refusal was on the grounds of sex or race (where compensation is unlimited), so great care must be taken in specifying the reason for the refusal and ensuring that it is one of those allowable (see Chapter 1).

One of the difficulties identified has been *getting employees to focus on the needs of the organisation,* as well as their own perceived rights. That is why reasonable time should be given to the meeting with the employee, so both sides understand the nature of the requests, the options available and the likely effect on the department, work colleagues and the business. One of the options is to agree to a change in hours or work for a limited trial basis to see if it works out. This must be confirmed in writing, because agreements made are regarded at law as permanent unless agreed otherwise at the time.

A further difficulty may arise if there are *conflicting requests*. Perhaps one request comes from an employee who is not currently protected under the law (say one with a caring responsibility not yet specified under the Act) and another comes from an employee with young children, who is therefore protected. In this case, it is wise to consider making it clear in written procedures that precedence will be given to those employees who are currently protected, even if it is considered that their case, although reasonable, is not quite so convincing.

Finally, a situation may arise where the organization does not believe it has *sufficient information* from the employee to be able to take a reasoned decision. It seems necessary to ask more questions or obtain more detailed evidence, perhaps about a disability. Here it is important to be aware of the employee's right to 'respect for private and family life' under the Human Rights Act, so the enquirer must not be too intrusive. On balance, it is advisable to accept the word of the employee on trust, but ensure that the request contains confirmation of his or her eligibility. In that way, if it comes to light that the employee has misled the employer, there may be grounds for disciplinary action (Hayden-Smith 2003).

Here is an example of the approach by the courts in the case of a domestic crisis. Qua had been absent on many occasions owing to her son's medical condition, and her employment was terminated after nine months' service. She appealed on the grounds of unfair dismissal. The Employment Appeals Tribunal dismissed her claim, stating that employees can only take emergency leave to arrange for a dependent to receive temporary help, and not to provide the care themselves, and certainly cannot take unlimited time off, even if they tell the employer on each occasion. This case therefore confirmed that the right to take emergency leave had limitations, depending on the nature of each case and circumstance.

The case also highlighted the need to keep a record of the date, length and reason for each absence and whether it had been authorised as dependant's leave. Source: Cooper (2003) on *Qua v John Ford Morrison* (2002 EAT/884/01).

SUPPORTING AND MANAGING THE SCHEMES

Most flexible working schemes depend on line managers to implement the detailed arrangements, enthuse the staff and handle any difficulties that arise. Persuading managers to accept non-standard working arrangements has been the biggest problem associated with flexible working, according to CIPD research (Coussey 2000). Organisations reported that managers assumed such changes would lead to problems, such as more complaints from customers and lower productivity, although the reverse appeared to be true in most cases. They were quite fearful of employees disappearing from the line of sight through home working and teleworking, and wondered how they could be managed properly. What led to acceptance was success on a small scale. If it can be seen to work in one area, then others see the positive results and the scheme sells itself.

The organisation has to be careful that the manager is not caught in the middle – faced with demands from above to meet targets and higher service levels, yet to go along with schemes that appear on the surface to give gains only to staff. Introducing multi-skilling or annualised hours can bring an extended period of disruption while staff learn how the scheme works and test it out, while the manager tries to ensure it is business as usual. Family-friendly improvements can lead to employees coming up with requests they would not have considered before the schemes were introduced, leading to very time-consuming discussions and scenario-planning on the manager's part to see if the employee's request can be met and at what cost.

On the other hand, many ideas for improvements on labour flexibility or managing hours have come from line managers. They have seen how time is wasted and the work flow distorted by the imbalance of skills available. They have also seen how peaks and troughs of production and service are not best met by staff on standard hours. Getting staff to initiate improvements can be the key to success, as shown by the Lloyds TSB case study.

In terms of persuading managers, Clutterbuck (2003) advocates three solutions:

- patient explanation of the personal and business benefits
- patient explanation and demonstration of the benefits to their department and team
- providing practical and relevant examples of solutions other managers have tried successfully – especially if they are presented by peers the target managers regard as credible.

Support of the trade union

In unionised environments, the support of trade unions is an essential ingredient for a successful outcome. At Blackburn and Darwen Council, for example, the support of Unison was essential in spreading the culture of

---

Case study 18: Management support for compressed hours at Lloyds TSB

Neil Hasson heads the small group manpower and information team at Lloyds TSB, which works within the bank's tight reporting cycle. Apart from regular reports for 50 business units, there is much urgent one-off work needed for senior executives, often carried out at very short notice. This is not naturally fertile ground for flexible working, with the initial concern that some team members might believe themselves to be carrying other colleagues who are taking advantage of various flexible hour systems.

Despite such doubts, in 1999 Hasson took a closer look at the concept of a compressed fortnight, with employees working 9 days out of 10 and adjusting their daily hours accordingly. He had seen a similar arrangement working elsewhere. The time off would kick in when the team was not working at its peak. The scheme was designed so there were no gaps at any time in the service the team offered to the organisation, and every team member had a valid role to play. Hasson took the proposal to the whole team, armed with a 10-page Q&A booklet that he hoped would anticipate all the problems. This proved an inspired move. Commitment from all the staff became easy to obtain, and the scheme has proved a success since implementation.

Source: Mahoney (2002).

---

empowerment and measuring outcomes, not hours. In one pilot scheme, the union took a major role in supporting management in encouraging the development of a self-rostering system for 70 staff in supported living units, and this worked extremely well in improving the morale of the staff and reducing grievances. In fact, the latter benefit reduced the union caseload to manageable levels (Tarpey 2004). Experience elsewhere has supported this view, with unions willing to give firm support to family-friendly benefits and agree to other new initiatives such as annualised hours if a good case is made and employees are protected (Coussey 2000).

Using trial periods

As indicated in a number of the cases, the use of a trial period is often an effective way of convincing managers and staff that a scheme can be successful. In Bristol-Myers Squibb, sales people were found to be generating more business once they had switched to a flexible hours arrangement that meant them working fewer hours in total, and this helped to overcome line managers' initial reluctance.

In the Nationwide Building Society, all flexible arrangements are first undertaken on a trial basis to help to assess their viability, with the trial lasting 13 weeks (IDS 2004b).

Training and development

For flexible working systems to gain credence throughout an organisation, the quality of training is highly significant. The training must help to embed a culture where flexible working is a natural process, rather than exceptional, and where an employee's performance is outcome-related rather than measured by the number of hours put in. Moreover, the culture must have sympathetic values and a willingness to share the successes and difficulties.

Developing such a culture is not easy. It is not helped if senior managers work long hours and appear to expect the same from their subordinates. Allowing meetings to drag on beyond 19:00, landing staff with urgent work that cannot be completed without late nights, arranging breakfast meetings and working lunches, all set the tone for expected employee behaviours. Under this culture, published policies and systems to encourage flexible working, especially work–life balance benefits, are regarded as mere platitudes or escapes for the unambitious. Training therefore has to be directed and supported from the top, and without that support the training is likely to be badly received and ineffective.

Where joined-up management exists and where policy and actual practice gel, however, innovate training can transmit the messages and invigorate the take-up level.

Effective training can take a number of forms. For employees to understand the way specialised initiatives work in areas such as annualised hours, teleworking or multi-skilling, specific training seminars need to be run. Depending on the complexity of the scheme, there will normally be dedicated management and supervision courses, dealing with running the operational aspects. Separate courses and seminars are normally put on for all other levels of employee affected by the scheme. To ensure understanding of the details, the course should be interactive. with case scenarios inserted and plenty of practical examples, such as how to deal with employees who refuse to be flexible within the rules, or what happens to hours on call-outs.

It is also worth considering joining the groups together so that the same message comes across to employees at all levels. Trainers know that some of the most enjoyable and effective sessions include role reversal, where employees learn to understand differing viewpoints by acting out the part of their superior or subordinate.

Where work–life balance issues are concerned, a number of organisations have linked the initiatives with training and communication in stress management. In this case the opportunities to work flexibly can form an outcome from employees' assessment of their own needs and context. Ford Europe, for example, has developed a series of innovative workshops and seminars which link stress management and healthy lifestyles with how individuals should manage their own working arrangements, and the family-friendly benefits they can buy into, such as career breaks and paternity leave (McCartney 2003).

The areas that are tackled, once employees understand the implications of a balanced lifestyle and the importance of effectively managing stress levels, cover:

- practical insights into their own work and life situations, using a diagnostic questionnaire

- examining how flexible working options and benefits operate, and any costs involved

- techniques for narrowing the options and deciding on the best course of action

- advice on how to discuss the process with line managers, colleagues and family members and reach an amicable solution.

Further supportive training for managers could cover areas such as engaging the team in working out flexible solutions to working problems, handling remote employees, relationships with complementary (temporary) employees, and developing a supportive climate for work–life balance.

Specific training is needed to support managers who have to take decisions in response to the statutory right to flexible working. Working through examples of identifying the impact of requests, understanding thoroughly the legislation, scenarios of collapsing five-day jobs into three-day jobs, what proportion of work can be done at home and how often the facility is granted, and ensuring that decisions are arrived at in a consistent and defensible way, are all important to line managers if they are to be trusted to take first-line decisions. It is so much better if they get this right, because decisions that are reversed on appeal deflate and undermine the manager, and encourage more appeals in the future.

Communication

Continuing to foster the culture of flexible working must be supported by a committed schedule of regular communication. This can be done through a variety of generic channels, such as the corporate intranet, internal magazines, team meetings and face-to-face presentations. At a large pharmaceutical company, a special effort is made during 'work–life balance week', which the company deliberately moved to May to coincide with the summer hours period, with its opportunity of compressed hours and an early finish on Friday. During this week, events are planned that seek to reinforce the message that work–life balance is a key element of the company's reward package. Each month, one aspect of the total package is picked as a theme to be spotlighted and promoted, with the emphasis on informing employees of the options open to them and encouraging them to think about ways of enhancing their own personal work–life balance (IDS 2004b).

For Tesco, the introduction of variations in its flexible working schemes centred around 'supporting your attendance', with the organisation, in addition to conventional communication media, using a poster competition and a high-level launch at the company's annual conference, with a senior retail director acting as champion on the day.

Most large organisations maintain a website to help all the staff understand the issues and to update them on developments. Abbey (formerly Abbey National) maintains a comprehensive set of intranet web pages covering all its policies and procedures. For example, it has 10 pages giving details on career breaks, including explanations of the two main schemes, eligibility, salary and benefits implications, and return to work arrangements.

Some organisations go into considerable detail to ensure that all parties are quite clear on where responsibilities lie. Table 5 is an extract from a large pharmaceutical company's intranet on responsibilities in respect of requests for flexible working.

Monitoring and evaluation

Regular revisits to flexible working schemes are essential. It has been repeated a number of times in this text that there needs to be a form of measurable target set when the scheme is initiated. Only if there are such targets can it be seen whether the schemes are successes or not. The measures can include:

- *Employee take-up of family-friendly schemes*, such as paternity leave, working from home and compressed hours. If the numbers are lower than expected, an investigation is required to find out why. If managers are inundated by requests, again an investigation is required to consider whether the terms of the schemes are right or whether they are too generous.

- *Turnover and absence analysis.* Improved flexible working should lead to greater employee motivation and commitment. If turnover and absence levels remain stubbornly high, the schemes have clearly failed. Similarly, if the levels drop for a period, then start to climb again, there is something wrong with the support mechanism.

- *Cost savings* in schemes such as annualised hours or outsourcing. Targets are easier to set here because they are normally at the heart of the decision to implement the scheme, so if the costs are not saved, the scheme has gone badly wrong. Not only have there been the disruption costs of change, there will also be considerable loss of management credibility if savings are not achieved. Another key point here is that, even if cost savings are made, the quality aspects of the product or service need to be maintained or improved. If quality or on-time delivery or customer satisfaction fall, there will be long-term difficulties. Monitoring these measures remains crucial here.

- *Staff satisfaction surveys.* Most organisations that have a belief in the power of staff motivation and commitment carry out regular staff satisfaction audits. Adding questions about flexible working practices and work–life balance can help the monitoring process and build up a view of the scheme's successes.

Special notes for small and medium-sized organisations (SMEs)

Issues surrounding flexibility may not be top of the agenda for smaller businesses, but flexible working is inherent in their operations, simply because they have fewer employees to do a standard number of jobs. Hence receptionists in small companies are always multi-tasked, for example acting as wages clerks and personnel administrators in part of their working time.

Research has indicated that SMEs often operate advanced flexible practices without clearly laying these down as 'policies'. This is especially true in the professional services sector, where staff needed to be adaptable, prepared to be on call, and willing to vary their part-time hours or work before or after their core hours (Bevan et al 1999).

Table 5 | **Responsibilities and accountabilities for requests to work flexibly**

Manager	Employee	Suggested action for all parties
Fully consider the request and whether the job can be carried out more flexibly. Immediately notify HR of the employee's request.	Fully consider the impact of the request on current job and how any issues may be overcome. Monitoring activities/timelines may assist this process. Could also consider involving colleagues in this process so that team continues to operate effectively.	Draw up a list of advantages and barriers of proposed flexible working. Notify HR of arrangement. Think through how the proposed working pattern could work.
Have an understanding of the flexible working policy and guidance.	Have an understanding of the flexible working policy and guidance.	
Accountability for delivering stated team/departmental objectives and must ensure that the organisational requirements are met. Consideration also needs to be given to the potential impact on the employee's personal objectives/career opportunities and how this can be managed.	Consider how the request may impact on personal circumstances/career. Demonstrate personal flexibility where feasible, eg be prepared to do extra hours during busy periods.	Demonstrate trust and commitment, as these are integral to the success of any flexible working arrangement. Consider actions that can be taken to encourage flexibility within the arrangement.
Identify impact of flexible working arrangements on employee, colleagues and clients.	Consider how the request may impact on colleagues and clients and how these may be overcome.	Agree how the arrangement will be communicated to colleagues and clients.

Table 5 | **Continued**

Manager	Employee	Suggested action for all parties
Discuss any employment legislation implications with HR.	Identify any changes to terms and conditions of employment with HR.	Discuss request with HR at the beginning of process or as early as possible.
Consider a trial period.	Consider a trial period.	Trial periods are normally for up to three months.
Responsible for setting performance objectives with the employee and reviewing on a regular basis.	Agree performance objectives with manager.	Set regular performance review dates.
As part of regular performance reviews, ensure that discussions occur around current and future circumstances (both parties) that may affect the flexible working arrangement.	Give advance notice of any changes in personal circumstances that may affect the existing flexible working arrangement.	Regular open and honest discussions.

For Classic Cleaners, a two-shop, 11-employee operation in Kingston, 'flexibility in working hours was key to our success – absenteeism disappeared almost overnight and staff turnover fell while business turnover went up 15 per cent' (Mahoney 2002).

Two further examples of flexible working in SMEs are given in case study 19.

Case study 19: Flexibility at Innocent Drinks and Castle Green Hotel

Innocent Drinks is a maker of totally natural fruit drinks, with only 40 staff and with a core value of ensuring that its staff are happy and productive. Work–life balance is encouraged through a flexible approach to starting and finishing hours and working at home, plus a number of more unusual initiatives. Newly-weds get a paid break of five days, sabbaticals are encouraged with a full guarantee of a job on return, and six £1,000 scholarships a year are offered towards the fulfilment of an ambition that is not work-related (IDS 2004b).

The Castle Green Hotel has 100 bedrooms. It is in Kendal in the Lake District, an area with less than 1 per cent unemployment, and had considerable retention difficulties before improving its flexible working initiatives. Employees now have a wide choice of flexible hours, leave options and career choices. Staff turnover has reduced by a half and there is currently 100 per cent return to work after maternity leave. In total £25,000 has been saved through the use of flexible working arrangements.

Source: cases kindly supplied by Work Life Balance Consultancy.

5

Selling the idea of flexible working and managing flexibility into your business

INTRODUCTION

Very few projects enjoy the luxury of starting from a clean slate. Flexible working usually reaches the company agenda in response to a challenge (such as legislative changes) or initiative (such as a desire to reduce costs through locating processes where they will be completed faster or for less outlay). Whatever the reason for considering flexible working, the usual first step is to build a solid business case. Having got this far in the book you will be familiar with the pros and cons of flexible working. Other people in your organisation may not be. Your job, if you are seeking to implement flexibility, is to focus on maximising the positive benefits, and ensure that potential drawbacks are identified and minimised.

If your flexibility scheme looks like generating more work for those impacted by it (for example, the IT support function will now have to implement shifts to cater for the non-standard working hours of flexible workers), you can expect to meet resistance. This chapter aims to ease your passage through the introductory phases, and highlights the likely 'sticking points' you might encounter.

WHO ARE YOUR STAKEHOLDERS?

Before you get into too much detail about which of the various practices outlined in this book you want to employ, it is worth stepping back and asking yourself this question. Typically you will find the following internal groups have a view:

- employee representatives
- employees

- line managers

- human resource administration

- the IT department.

In addition you may have numerous customer and supplier groups to consider. For each of these groupings you will need to research at the basic level: what it is they need from flexibility, what aspects they are happy to support and what aspects they would object to.

INFLUENCING THE DIFFERENT GROUPS

Whenever you are trying to influence people to change there are a number of key stages to go through. The underlying principle is that people are much more likely to support your ideas if they buy in, through being involved and consulted fully in the early stages of the process. Trying to put across your ideas on flexible working implementation will be much more successful if you become competent at each of the stages.

Before you start trying to influence others, you must be sure that moving to flexible working is really the right thing to do. The only way you can be sure is to conduct preparatory background research into the needs of each of the stakeholders you are targeting. The first stage in the influencing process is to get 'under the skin' of the person you are trying to influence. You will need to know what his or her challenges are, what his or her priorities are, how he or she is currently experiencing problems and what he or she feels about a range of issues related to the areas under discussion. The technical term for this stage in the process is 'pacing'.

Pacing can take various forms, such as interviewing, focus groups, questionnaires, and observation, but it is really an information-gathering exercise to find out both facts and feelings about the surrounding issue, the people involved, and anything and anyone who is connected to it. Obviously this could take a long time, so you may have to limit your research once you feel you have enough to move forward.

The next stage, once you feel you have a good grasp of the general situation facing your 'client' and the areas involved, is to make some more detailed enquiries about how things might be improved. Again the techniques involved focus on questioning and interviewing, but until this stage is complete it is not possible to make an effective diagnosis, which is where you can begin to formulate your flexible working approach.

This diagnosis stage of the influencing process really starts with your consideration of the information you have obtained and analysed, with a view to deciding the nature of the problems and challenges you have unearthed. Using the term 'diagnosis' is really quite appropriate, as you can take the approach that would typically be taken in a medical analysis, where the first thing to decide is whether the situation that has been unearthed represents a curable problem or is more accurately described as a 'condition' (that is, it is not going to change much whatever you do). If it is the former, you can start your journey into flexible working by aiming to cure the problems currently being experienced. If your research leads you to believe that the situation you are working with is more likely to be a condition, your flexible working approach will need to be geared more towards problem alleviation than cure.

Once you have made your initial diagnosis, it is generally worth returning to key stakeholders and double-checking that you have not missed something out, or misunderstood what was said earlier in your investigation. If this proves to be the case, or new factors have emerged in the interim, you will obviously need to alter your analysis accordingly. It might be a good idea to publish an interim report or 'white paper' for broader discussion at this stage. You can then take feedback on your report and incorporate it into the next phases.

By now you should be feeling confident enough to start generating expectations of what might be achievable by applying some of the flexible working practices and principles we have been talking about in this book. Care is needed at this stage that in your anxiety to generate enthusiasm you do not over-commit and set yourself up for failure at a later stage. It is always better to under-promise and over-deliver than the other way round. What is needed is some leading of people into thinking about the possibilities and options available from increasing or introducing flexibility.

The next stage in the influencing process is to offer some proposals for discussion or consideration. Some of these will be rejected, some will need to be revised, and some might go straight to action, so you need to be ready to take any or all of these responses from your stakeholders. The key thing here is to be offering options rather than complete 'take it or leave it' solutions.

The final stage in the influencing process should be straightforward if all the preceding stages have worked well. The need to persuade people to action or to sign off permission to go ahead with your flexible working proposal will always be more difficult if you are not able to work through the stages of influencing outlined above.

Of course the major drawback of taking this staged approach is the time it takes. When situations demand faster responses you cannot use this model of influencing, and may have to resort to more direct approaches, and try to minimise the attendant problems these often have.

SELLING THE KEY BENEFITS OF FLEXIBILITY

When any radical organisational change is proposed there is often a natural tendency by some to resist and ask questions like 'Why are we doing this?' and 'If this is such good idea why didn't we think of it before?' To quickly get beyond this it is important to remember that flexible working is not the *raison d'être* of the organisation. It is merely a way of helping to achieve its objectives and goals. This means you might have to change your tack from selling flexibility in itself, to selling the sustainable benefits it promises to deliver.

Obviously, any gains in customer satisfaction, operational efficiency, cost reduction and employee motivation will be uppermost, and these can form central planks of the business case for flexibility. But do not forget the potential of flexible working in other areas such as harnessing creativity and innovation.

Richard Florida (2002) has presented research findings from his work into creativity, and is in no doubt that flexible working environments stimulate and promote the ability to do things differently. He equates the opportunity to work flexibly with freeing up the minds of the employees. If you consider the most creative professions such as artists or musicians, think about the environments they work in. Typically an artist's studio is not a regimented workplace. It might well look like total chaos from the outside. I remember once being struck by the mess and general untidiness of the design offices of one of the most creative marketing companies I have ever come across, Big Stick Advertising and Marketing, based in Tring, England. Yet whenever I have asked its staff to provide creative input to a project, I have been consistently impressed with the quality and difference that they bring to concepts. They are living proof that what some would call 'chaotic' environments do yield creative and innovative outputs.

Why is it then that when we want corporate researchers to be creative and innovative we tend not to replicate this type of environment? Two exceptions to this were reported by Whyte (1956), who commented that two R&D labs were conspicuous by their ability to achieve a far higher rate of discovery than any others. These were the labs of General Electric and Bell Labs. They were coincidentally famous for encouraging individualism, patience with off-the-wall ideas, and being least likely to operate as closely monitored, tightly controlled, inflexible project teams.

Flexibility can also yield major benefits where organisations are experiencing difficulties in recruiting people into these more creative areas. Florida (2002) quotes an US *Information Week* Salary Survey from 2001, which claimed from evidence collected on 20,000 IT workers that flexibility was the second most important factor in deciding whether they wanted to work for a company. This factor was second only to 'the challenge offered by the work' and actually more important than both 'job stability' and 'pay'. Florida, (2002) confirmed this view with his own research, claiming that people in his focus groups blanched at the very mention of a nine-to-five schedule or a standard dress code.

> *How you use your time and how you dress and adorn yourself are intensely personal aspects of life. People are no longer willing to compromise on these matters simply to get a job. Many spoke of 'wanting to bring themselves to work.'*
>
> *(Florida 2002)*

Florida does acknowledge that the move toward increased flexibility will probably favour smaller organisations, and that large corporations with their self-imposed bureaucratic procedures and deeply entrenched rule-bound behaviours will continue to struggle to incorporate the maverick creatives. This is often the reason that IT, marketing and R&D functions, where there is a need to attract less conventional employees, are located out of the way of other parts of the organisation or customer-facing functions. Hiding away these 'unruly children', who are actually driving much of the development of product or service, means they are not allowed to disrupt the more conventional parts of the organisation which do not need the same flexibility and would not fully understand the implications.

This too can be turned into a major opportunity. If you can use flexible working practices in your organisation to capture the benefits of being small, your chances of improving competitive ability against larger market players will be enhanced.

Selling flexibility to senior managers and line managers

The chief resistance factors here are likely to focus around a fear of the unpredictability or inconsistency of service that might result from flexible working, and at least an element of lost control, particularly if the person concerned is highly structured and change-averse. These factors need to be countered by evidence to show that the flexibility proposed will actually ensure a more complete service, and will be at least no less reliable than current measures. Concerns around control will also need to be addressed at an early stage, as senior managers have enough risks to deal with over day-to-day matters. The last thing they want is to have any further risks imposed by flexible working. This means you must demonstrate clearly that you have considered back-up plans, contingencies and scenarios where various problems might arise, and processes to counter them.

Often a good tactic here is to highlight successes that other, competitor organisations are having with flexibility. Or if you feel you are going to be the first in your market to adopt flexible working practices, can you somehow quantify the premium you expect to extract from being a flexible working pioneer?

Selling flexibility to employees

Employees who are being asked to move into a more flexible working environment may need to be convinced of the advantages for them alongside those for the organisation. Again it is best to sell the benefits and not the concept. This book has contained numerous examples of employees who are able to achieve a better work–life balance, and improve their own productivity by working flexibly. Nonetheless there will be groups for whom flexible working is not instantly welcome, and this must be recognised.

Some of the possible downsides about flexible working from an employee perspective are:

- less predictable working commitments

- variability in income (depending on the flexibility model used)

- less predictable social interaction with regular customers and teammates.

Some people will resist the change from fear of the unknown and uncertainty about how they will be affected. Clear and full communications and consultation with those affected will help. In our experience some typical concerns that employees have about flexible working are:

- Will I be expected to work longer or more unsocial hours than I currently do?

- Will I get the right technological support?

- What will be the tax and income implications for me of the change?

- Am I insured for company property on my premises?

- How will I be communicated with and kept up to date with things when I am not around?

- How will I be able to maintain the level of social contact that I currently enjoy at work?

Because flexibility programmes are so varied, each of the above and other concerns, will need to be addressed on a case by case basis. Thought needs to be put into how the established methodology of working and managing employees will be redesigned to ensure that the benefits of flexibility are sustained and the drawbacks avoided.

Companies need to introduce any flexible working programme in a planned, coordinated way so that objections and difficulties highlighted by particular employees or groups can be handled in a professional and effective manner. Forcing flexible working onto employees who do not see any benefits and appear to be experiencing only the downsides is a recipe for reduced motivation, poor application and built-in failure.

Using the services of a flexible working consultant

One way of assessing and implementing flexible working options for many organisations is to look at buying in support from outside. There are a range of experts (for example the authors of this book!) able to work on projects aimed at increasing or developing flexibility, to provide an extra resource to organisations where the need for flexibility is clear but staff do not really know how to approach it.

Flexible working consultants should be able to guide you through the whole process, from looking at where flexibility would be most beneficial to how it should be addressed. They will also be able to warn you of the pitfalls. A good consultant will generally save you more that he or she costs you, in time saved in reaching your flexible working goals and in error avoidance. Ideally you need someone who has some experience in the industry sector relevant to your organisation. For a good start in seeking advice on flexible working, look on the website www.knowledgedoctor.com, where further information about a range of flexible working, and knowledge-based working issues can be found.

CHANGING THE ROLE OF HR TO ACCOMMODATE FLEXIBLE WORKING

The HR function can be a real driving force behind flexible working. It can also cause it to stall. Depending on the motivation behind the move towards flexibility, the HR role will differ. Table 6 lists the major issues.

The issues identified suggest that the HR role in preparing for,

Table 6 | **HR roles in flexible working**

Motivation for flexible working	Possible contribution from HR	Extending the value of the HR role	Possible snags and pitfalls for the HR function	Other comments
Reduced costs/ increased efficiency.	Providing management information on labour costs. Leading contract change negotiations.	Research into alternative forms of flexibility and their impact.	Being seen as the 'flexibility police'.	This is a real opportunity to place HR services at the heart of a business development initiative.
Improve/ extend customer service.	Provide management information on employee availability and preferences over shift patterns or changes.	As above.	Difficult to measure how the flexibility will lead to increased service satisfaction.	Ties the HR function to a real business problem area.
Response to requests from employees.	Provide guidance on the consequences of sanctioning the request.	As above plus tie in flexible working preferences to reward and compensation packages.	Could open a floodgate of requests that cannot be satisfied.	Opportunity to innovate and improve work–life balance.
Compliance with legislation/ regulations.	Up-to-date guidance on the current position and health and safety issues.	Share good practice with diverse business units. Share lessons learned.	Again difficult to avoid the policing approach.	As above.

incorporating and maintaining flexible working practices can not be over-estimated. Non-HR managers will naturally look to the function to help them address the range of problems and opportunities on offer.

This naturally means a shift in emphasis for the more traditional HR area. HR professionals faced with demands from all sides to improve flexibility will need to consider their own skill sets and what needs to be done to provide the required support. As a minimum, the HR function now needs to become familiar with what is available, what technological advances are expected and what the advantages and disadvantages of each of the flexible working options discussed in this book would be for their internal and external client base.

More adventurous departments might consider pioneering the approaches themselves, and trialling some of the flexible working models that we have seen. Often the need is to act as a quasi-consultant to ensure that whatever flexible working solutions are proposed and implemented actually meet the needs of the organisation alongside those of the employees and managers affected. Beyond this, many organisations will also see their HR resource as facilitating the introduction and monitoring progress with flexibilisation.

Depending on the size of the operation, the move to flexible working may need to be a staged process, and here the central HR function can act as a good practice depository, and advise those in later phases of the changes on what to look out for.

QUANTIFYING THE BENEFITS OF FLEXIBLE WORKING

While each case will be unique, it is possible to learn from others, so here are some of the benefits that other companies have found from implementing flexible working programmes.

- Effective and efficient client delivery – operations can now really be 'open 24/7', as telephones can be answered by home workers or those in different time zones.

- Call centres can improve the response to customers by appropriate filtering and diverting calls during busy periods to 'overcapacity sites'.

- Mobile staff can be in contact for longer with their customer base as they do not need to travel to and from fixed bases.

- Staff can be located close to suppliers or source markets to take advantage of information or changes instantly.

- Lower operating costs, reduced premises or less floorspace, shared desks and so on.

Many of the gains from flexibility are by their very nature difficult if not impossible to quantify. Here it is down to the skill of the management team to determine how to extract the most from flexibility gains. For example if the flexibility programme yields an opportunity to use one less floor of space in a building, this is no real benefit unless the space can be surrendered for gain, or another use found for it. In this instance the organisation might, for example, bring staff in from another location, perhaps at the end of its lease, or use the space to provide an improved facility such as a new canteen or crêche. This would not save any money but it might still be a real benefit made possible by flexible working.

In a similar way using flexibility to save employee time only improves productivity if managers are able to access this saved time and put it to work in other areas. This is a point that often gets overlooked if HR is just asked to implement flexibility without the line manager being involved.

More simple cost calculations can be made from figures like time travelled to and from work. For most employees this is a cost borne personally, so the company will not see any direct payback on its balance sheet. But if the goodwill and job satisfaction generated by a travel time saving of two hours per day per employee results in greater time and effort going into positive work activity, that must be a benefit.

Attracting and retaining staff might also be a hidden benefit of flexible working. For some people the work–life balance made possible by flexible working is a key aspect of their reward package. Reducing labour turnover, with its attendant costs of training, advertising and recruitment activity and the low productivity of new hires, will therefore be an indirect benefit of introducing flexible working.

If any of the above apply to your situation, you should be able to do some quick rough reckoning of the amounts of time or money that would be involved, to help you put together the business case for flexible working.

EQUAL OPPORTUNITIES AND ENVIRONMENTAL ISSUES AROUND FLEXIBLE WORKING

Most large organisations these days have ethical and environmentally friendly policy statements, as the topic of corporate responsibility is high on the agenda these days. The introduction of flexible working has a real role to play here, in that home workers do not have to 'commute and pollute'. Flexibility also allows greater access to employment for those who are less able to travel, and prevents the overcrowding of already high-cost locations.

It could even be claimed that it is socially responsible to take work to the workers rather than the other way around, by locating employment opportunities (perhaps from a new call centre) in economically deprived areas.

PLANNING YOUR WAY: MAKING FLEXIBLE WORKING HAPPEN

In a typical scenario the HR manager is asked either to investigate the possibilities for flexible working to benefit the organisation, or maybe worse, simply to implement flexible working. This guide considers a few steps along the way.

First stage: feasibility study

What should be done?

First, investigate what could be done. What is the appetite amongst those likely to be affected? Be careful not to raise expectations, as if your flexibility scheme does not take off, you might have to deal with disappointed people. Do some preliminary costings, weighed against the likely benefits of flexibilisation.

Who needs to be involved?

You will probably need to convene a project team once the project is firmly under way, but at this early stage it may be sufficient to ensure you consult with:

- external technology suppliers and maintainers
- the in-house technology function to see what their concerns are over issues like security and support
- representatives of the functions to be flexibilised
- the facilities/premises manager, to see if alternative use could be made of any freed-up space
- other people in the organisation who have been through similar programmes.

Only if the feasibility study looks positive should you move into the next phase.

Second stage: prepare the business case

What should be done?

Prepare your case by outlining the need for flexibility. This need is generally more impactful if it comes from pressing business problems like an inability to meet demand or low customer satisfaction with the current provision. Alternatively it could come from pressure on employees, difficulty in recruiting or retaining staff, or it could simply be a legislative requirement.

What else should be in the case proposal?

Typically once you have justified the need for flexibility, executives will want to see clear costings up-front. At this stage you may need to use some creativity, but base your costings on evidence from similar projects whenever possible. These costings should be detailed enough to indicate when the costs would be incurred.

After the costing you should outline the expected benefits. Where possible attach a monetary figure to them but if a benefit is not quantifiable simply say so, or use proxy measures such as 'staff motivation'. Again, do not forget to include estimates of when these expected benefits will accrue.

Once these sections are completed you should be able to present a payback period as part of the business case. In your favour here is the fact that much of the investment in flexible working is front-loaded while the returns should be ongoing. This means that over a five-year period you should be able to estimate steady returns with only marginal increases in investment in support for flexible working.

Third stage: pilot approach

A typical next step is to go with a pilot in a small area of the organisation, and look to extract maximum learning from this with a view to rolling out the flexibilisation project.

The pilot should be used to test assumptions on costs and benefits. It will also give you the chance to estimate what sort of project team will be required to implement flexible working in the future. All learning from the pilot should be logged and shared. It is a good idea to set up a flexible working project intranet site, so that other managers and employees who are interested can see the development for themselves.

POSSIBLE FUTURE SCENARIOS FOR FLEXIBLE WORKING

To complete this text we thought it would be good, if a little risky, to speculate on the likely future prospects for flexible working. We have detailed the practical aspects of organising for flexibility in the foregoing chapters. We believe that flexible working has so many advantages, for employer and employee alike, that much of what we have covered will soon become normal working practice.

Nonetheless there may be some areas of business and the economy where ongoing resistance and restrictions on flexibility mean that many of these benefits are not achieved. In the following scenarios you will see some of our ideas on what flexibility may mean in the next few years.

Scenario 1 Flexibility: what's the alternative?

We have seen already that the UK already has over 5,000 call centres, mostly providing examples of flexible employment, demonstrating that flexibility can be made to work in large-scale service operations. In addition we have seen, in many developed economies, the demise of the 'one company career'. Add to this the increasing desire for a better work–life balance, and the prospects for flexible working look bright.

The prospect of enjoying no flexibility in the workplace would be enough to discourage even an application from many potential recruits. As we have seen from the case studies in this book, most people who have experienced working flexibly show no desire to revert to traditional fixed employment models.

Flexible working is increasingly supported by the technological advances in communications that continue to speed up and broaden connectivity, meaning that work can find the employee more easily than before, and the truly location-independent worker is far more possible than most people think.

In some countries legislation is also being proposed to encourage flexible working for a range of political and economic reasons. Local and national governments can see the clear macroeconomic benefits of flexible working feeding through into areas such as less traffic congestion, healthier populations who suffer less stress, and greater opportunities for those who cannot contribute to the working world in a full-time capacity.

Combining these features makes us believe that the traditional (that is, non-flexible) employment model will soon become the alternative, and the hitherto unusual practice of working flexibly will become the norm. The ultimate destination of this scenario will be the development of a flexible 'cyber world' where the opportunities of flexible working are really given their head. These opportunities might at first be restricted to an elite band of those qualified and technically competent, but history is full of examples where such technological barriers are overcome. In the short time since its inception the World Wide Web and all that it entails have changed irreversibly the way the world lives and works. The technology train has long since left the station; for some it is just a question of catching up with it.

No accurate estimate has been made of the proportion of work currently done that could easily be transferred to this 'cyber world', free from specific location or time, but it seems to us that counting the jobs that could not be delivered in some flexible manner will soon become a much easier task.

Scenario 2 Fast track, slow track

An alternative way that flexible working could develop could be an extension of what we can already observe. Some sectors within particular industries have already raced ahead and developed their preferred models of flexible working, while others are yet to realise how they too can tap into the benefits we have outlined in this book. With this 'dual-track' approach the inevitable consequence is a division of companies into winners and losers in the race for flexibility.

Those companies that are able to deploy and implement flexible working practices stand to benefit on both the supply and demand side. In terms of supply they will gain from having access to a wider pool of talent. They can use their approach to flexible working as a selling tool for attracting applications, and typically generate greater employee loyalty than companies where employment conforms very much to the standard nine-to-five model.

On the demand side, flexible working will allow the company on this track to tailor its product and service delivery to varying customer needs. As well as being able to offer 24/7 availability of service when needed, the ability to easily and efficiently flex output to meet variable demand according to seasonal or special event peaks and troughs will also pay dividends.

Coping with the storm of change witnessed in most markets will inevitably be less of a struggle where the key resources of the company can be flexed in the ways we have described in this book. Those organisations that ride the other track, whereby they are unable to cope with working in a flexible world and cannot cope with the mechanisms or challenges this presents, will be seriously hampered in their development.

Our view is that the flexible working genie is already out of the bottle, and the companies that remain on the non-flexible track will find the performance gap between them and the companies that do deploy flexible working slowly but inexorably widening, however it is measured. Flexibility, like nuclear weapons, cannot be 'uninvented'. We hope that this book has been a valuable addition to those managers considering and at some point implementing flexible working practices.

CONCLUSION

This chapter has shown you some clear, practical steps towards implementation of flexible working. Like all change in organisations it is not always an easy thing to accomplish. The closer you can tie the move toward flexible working to real business or employee needs, the more chance you will have of achieving what you want.

Remember that flexible working, with all the technological and behavioural changes it requires, is merely a toolkit for improving the way the organisation currently operates. How managers choose to deploy these tools will ultimately determine whether the eventual results of flexible working are good or bad.

Appendix

A bluffer's guide to talking IT in relation to HR

INTRODUCTION

This section is intended to quickly upskill any HR person who needs to communicate with a counterpart in an IT-related field. This is a generally both a highly likely and a highly problematic exercise. Many IT experts are renowned for having little patience in communicating with non-IT literate colleagues. Unfortunately you will need their support, understanding and maybe even permission to get your flexible working initiatives off the ground, so you will need to show at least a rudimentary knowledge of what technology is all about.

In addition, when one of your flexible working colleagues has an IT-related problem you may need to know enough to work out how it can be routed to a solution. There really is no way out of this except for the HR function to develop some understanding of basic IT language and conventions. This very brief alphabetical guide is just that. At the end of the guide are some useful suggestions of other places to look if you want to know more.

Active server pages (ASP (T))	A technique for generating webpages from a template held on a server. ASP can be used to automatically extract information from a database, format it as HTML and send it to a browser. ASP is especially useful for automatically updating reports where the core structure seldom changes but content often does.
ActiveX	Microsoft's ActiveX technology is used to make interactive webpages that look and behave like computer programs, rather than static pages. With ActiveX, users can use push buttons and interact in other ways with the webpage.

Applet	A small computer program dedicated to a specific task. Applets are often built into webpages to perform functions such as displaying animations or performing calculations.
Application service provider (ASP (T2))	A commercial provider (host) of server space for the delivery of applications via the Web.
Archive	1) To separate and store data for a long period of time. 2) A collection of data being stored for a long period of time.
Asymmetric digital subscriber line (ASDL)	A successor to ISDN, ASDL is used to transfer voice and data over the same communication line.
Avatar	A software program that stimulates a real person either physically or iconically. The most famous avatar to date is Ananova, the virtual newsreader.
Back up	To store data in a separate file and/or on a separate drive/device for the purpose of enabling recovery should the original data become lost or damaged.
Bandwidth	The capacity of a communications channel to pass data between systems, expressed as a number of units over a specified period of time (eg bits per second).
Bits per second (bps)	The number of bits (an elementary data item) that can be transferred from one place/computer to another in a second of time. Most descriptions of bandwidth are measures of bps.
Banner	The most common form of Web advertising. Usually in the form of a GIF image, most banners contain animations designed to catch the viewer's attention and links (click-throughs) to take them to the sponsor's site.
Blackberry	A hand-held device that allows users to access e-mails remotely (while away from their PC).
Browser	1) A software program that runs on the client machine and is used to interpret and display the data that websites send when accessed. 2) A PC program (software) that is used to contact and represent file data retrieved from an Internet server (website) according to an input destination name (URL) which has been converted to a numeric address (IP address) by a domain

name server (DNS). The source information retrieved is normally presented to the browser software in HTML form but, via incorporated 'plug-in' software modules and attachments to existing office automation programs, a large number of text, image, video and sound files or objects may also be presented automatically to the user. 3) A PC program that is used to retrieve and present file data extracted from an Internet website (server).

Business to employee (B2E)
An e-business term for transactions between businesses and their staff via Web-based technologies. Typical B2E transactions include expense claim processing, appraisals and automated pay.

C++
A programming language based on C or C enhanced to support object orientation. Developed by Bell Labs in the 1980s, C++ is still widely regarded as one of the best languages to address large-scale projects, albeit JAVA (another object-oriented language) is seen by many as easier to use.

Chat room
A place on the Internet where people go to 'chat' with other people in a virtual room. There are thousands of chat rooms across the Internet, usually organised by subject and often using images selected by participants ('avatars') to provide anonymity. All of the conversations taking place within the room may be viewed by all, unless a participant chooses to enter a private chat room established, and decorated, by one of the participants.

Cookie
A piece of information sent by an Internet website to a web browser. The browser software is expected to save and send back details to the website server. Cookies can be used to gather more information about a user and his or her PC. Cookies are usually saved in the PC memory until the browser software is closed down, but can be deleted at any time.

Cracker
An individual who attempts to gain unauthorised access to a system by breaking security codes.

Cybrarian
A librarian or researcher specialising in the Internet, rather than books, as a source of information.

Data compromise
The exposure of systems and information to unauthorized access.

Data matching	A technique in which sections of databases are matched against other information to try to match identical records. It does not apply to in-house matching exercises. It is aimed at matches made with information from a different legal entity or organisation.
Degauss	To permanently remove data from a magnetic storage medium.
Domain name	The highest-level name of the web site. For example, the name for HSBC Holdings plc within the .com global domain is hsbc.com. An Internet domain name is a unique name that identifies an Internet information site or host server. Any site may have several names. Domain names always have two or more parts separated by dots – a fully qualified domain name. The part on the left is the most specific, and the part on the right is the most general (eg name.com), usually one of the five original global Internet 'root' domains (.com, .org, .mil, .edu, .net) in which registrations are managed, for the moment, by US company Network Systems Inc (InterNIC) for the Internet community. Most countries have national domain registration groups – NICs (network information centres) – that allocate suffixed domain names (eg name.co.uk) for those wanting a less global appearance. If you type hsbc.com in the location area on your browser, you will be connected to the group's web site.
Domain name server	A computer system used to 'resolve' domain names into the numeric IP addresses which are actually used to direct Internet and intranet connections. Every Internet and intranet device has a unique IP address within some wider addressing convention. Like all other servers on the Internet, a DNS server may be attached anywhere on the network structure, but is usually provided as an ISP or internal corporate service.
Download	The transfer of information from an Internet site to an individual computer, usually using FTP (the file transfer protocol). Each time you instruct your computer system to retrieve your mail, the mail file is transferred to the mail agent in your computer. In this case special mail protocols (SMTP and POP) are used rather than FTP protocol.

Dynamic host configuration protocol (DHCP)   Each computing device attached to the Internet or an intranet requires a unique IP address within an addressing scheme to minimise conflicts. These may be assigned manually or automatically using a lease concept with a controllable time period. DHCP is the protocol that provides a means to allocate IP addresses within the assigned range to PCs on a local area network.

E-business   The process of conducting business over the Internet. It goes beyond e-commerce to incorporate a wide variety of business processes. These might take the form of maintaining inventories, showing product catalogues, tracking orders, and literally dozens of other business processes that were previously conducted in more traditional ways.

Encryption   A process that 'scrambles' a message so that it cannot be read by anyone other than the intended recipient.

Extranet   Use of Internet software (eg a web browser) and protocols over private networks, but where information and services are available for use both by the organisation and third parties (such as customers).

File transfer protocol (FTP)   1) FTP provides a means to log in to another Internet website, usually established specifically for that purpose, for retrieving, purchasing and/or transferring files of information (software, text, graphics, photo images, sound or video clips). 2) Internet standard protocol for moving data files from one computer to another.

Firewall   1) A dedicated PC hardware and software unit that provides a separation or gateway between two LANs across which IP network protocol traffic is examined, passed, rejected or directed for security purposes. Transport protocols other than IP (eg IBM's LLC2) are not examined or passed. Application layer protocols which provide Internet services or application functionality are transported using IP and may be passed or blocked depending on the functionality of the firewall product selected. 2)An Internet gateway that restricts data communication traffic to and from one of the connected networks (the one said to be 'inside' the firewall) and thus protects that network's system resources against threats from the other network (the one that is said to be 'outside' the firewall).

Flame/flaming This has come to refer to any excess of derogatory comment, no matter how witless or crude, generally conveyed by e-mail.

Frequently asked questions (FAQ) An organised list of frequently asked questions, with the answers provided. FAQs usually serve as a mini-help file. Similarly bulletin boards offer a service for a community of interest or expertise to answer questions from that community, presenting question and the several answers initiated in an organised fashion.

Graphic Interchange Format (GIF) A common format for pictures, graphics, backgrounds and photo image files, especially suitable for images containing large areas of the same colour. GIF format files of simple images are often smaller than the same file would be if stored in JPEG format, but GIF format does not store photographic images as well as JPEG.

Hypertext A text string on a web page that links the user to another page on the same site or to another site. The hypertext or hypertext links, by convention, are usually underlined and a different colour than the other text on the page.

Hypertext mark-up language (HTML) HTML is not a programming language; it is more akin to word processing document formatting. The manner in which the base text is to appear is described by HTML commands surrounding the text.

Hypertext transfer protocol (http://) The protocol that is used between browser software and website server to retrieve HTML page information. A browser will assume use of HTTP by default. Other protocols may be used by software tasks within a browser to obtain other information from the Internet such as mail messages or file information.

Internet service provider (ISP) ISPs provide a service by allowing subscribers to connect to the ISP's local area network as if the subscriber was using a workstation on the ISP premises. They provide a bridge to all the other LANs that together comprise the Internet. ISPs usually aim to provide several other services in order to attract custom, typically including mail hosting and advertising.

Interoperability The degree to which two or more software or hardware components work together.

Intranet 1) A form of network where the server is located within a specific defined organisation, and access is restricted to recognised persons within that entity. Use of internet software (eg web browser) and protocols over private networks where information and services are only available internally within a single organisation. 2) A private network inside a company or organisation that uses the same kind of technology, browser software, web server software and communication protocol (TCP/IP) as is found on the public Internet, but is aimed only at internal corporate use. The term is starting to be used very loosely for any internal corporate network, no matter how information is presented, accessed or conveyed.

JavaScript A scripting language, somewhat unrelated to Java (a programming language), whose functions are mainly limited to controlling the appearance of a document or the browser window.

Joint Photographic Experts Group (JPEG) Commonly used as a file storage/compression format for image files. For photographic images JPEG format is more efficient than the GIF format used for line art or simple logo art.

Link/hypertext link Text within a web page which covers the destination URL of another location within the same site or a different website altogether. Links can be text or graphic. Text links are usually underlined and are often a different colour from the rest of the text on the screen.

Local area network (LAN) A network that links nearby computers to one another.

Local systems administrator (LSA) Individual responsible for administration of the LAN/local system.

Logical partition (LPAR) A facility to consolidate multiple workloads into a single mainframe or server. Each logical partition is endowed with its own processor(s) and other virtual resources, and runs independently from the rest. With some systems you can dynamically share resources (load balancing) and communicate at high speeds among logical partitions.

Logon	A user sign-on/validation process. A successful logon involves a user entering a valid name and a password before access is granted.
Modulator-demodulator (modem)	Modems fool the telephone network, configured technically around the frequency ranges of the human voice, into believing that the encoded frequency signals used to represent data are voice. The data rate achieved by any modem for any call depends on very complex multi-level encoding using several frequencies, signal phase and amplitude shifts, and on the underlying quality of the telephone line.
Multipurpose internet mail extensions (MIME)	The standard for attachment of non-text files to Internet e-mail messages. Hence 'MIME sweep' is often used to denote sweeping attachments to e-mail messages for viruses and other agents prejudicial to a PC or internal system's operation. Non-text files include graphics, spreadsheets, formatted word-processor documents and sound files. Besides e-mail software, the MIME standard is also universally used by website servers to identify the files they are sending to browsers. In this way new file formats can be accommodated simply by updating the browsers' associations between MIME types and the appropriate 'plug-in' or software module for handling that particular file type.
Networked information centre (NIC)	Generally, any authority (self-assumed or appointed) that handles name registration and associated IP address linkages for Internet use. The most well known is InterNIC, the root domain registration service operated on behalf of the US government by Network Systems Inc. Elsewhere, typically a university or government agency or telecom authority will take this role.
Newsgroups	Ongoing discussion groups among people on the Internet who share a mutual interest, also called usenets.
Personal digital assistant (PDA)	A hand-held computing device that helps people manage information.
SAP	Based in Germany, SAP is a market and technology leader in client/server enterprise application software.
Secure electronic transactions (SET)	A collection of software algorithms built into most browsers to enable the security of financial transactions on the Internet.

Simple mail transport protocol (SMTP)	While POP3 is the protocol which allows e-mail to be retrieved from a POP3 host, SMTP is the protocol which allows e-mail to be sent to others. The SMTP (send) server which receives e-mail may, or may not be the same as the POP3 (receive) server which delivers it to the recipient.
Spam (or spamming)	Use of Internet e-mail as if it was a broadcast medium by sending the same message to a large number of people who did not ask for it. Usually unwelcome and inappropriate behaviour, likely to earn a considerable degree of flaming in return.
Taxonomy	The term is borrowed from biology and is not specific to computing. In the context of computing, taxonomy involves the hierarchical classification of artefacts.
Uniform resource locator (URL)	1) The address of a Web page, file or graphic stored on a Web-based network (WWW, intranet, LAN). 2) The text string given to a browser to identify the protocol to be used for information retrieval (eg 'http://', usually assumed by default), the Internet (website) server by domain name, and the page and section information required.
Virtual machine (VM)	In the VM environment, individual 'users' (or virtualised servers) can make use of a large mainframe or other computer, and the operating system will maintain the illusion to the user that the computer's resources are reflective of only the single virtualised server. The virtual machine can be customised to access particular resources independently of other demands being placed on the computer.
Wide area network (WAN)	A network that covers a more geographically widespread client base than a LAN.
Website	A personal/commercial/public location or site on the World Wide Web (WWW) consisting of one or more pages of information and data encoded to make them readable by a web browser.
Wireless application protocol (WAP)	A technology/set of specifications designed to give users access to the Web via PDAs (WAP enabled phones/PDAs/palm tops).
Zip	1)A popular type of compression technology used to shrink PC files before transmitting them across a network or storing them on a disk/drive. 2)A commonly used format for distributing software on the Internet.

OTHER USEFUL PLACES TO LOOK

The Telework Association web pages are found at www.telework.org.uk.

The pages of www.it-analysis.com give excellent figures and research on telecoms infrastructure.

References, further information and contacts

REFERENCES

ACCENTURE (2003) *Outsourcing in government: pathways to value.* London: Accenture.

ADVISORY CONCILIATION AND ARBITRATION SERVICE (ACAS) (1988) *Annualised Hours.* London: ACAS.

BAXTER INTERNATIONAL (2000) *Flexible Working,* October. 11–14.

BEVAN, S., DENCH, S., TAMKIN, P. and CUMMINS, J. (1999) *Family-friendly employment: the business case.* DfEE Research report, RR 136.

BIBBY, A. (2000) Wise council: Surrey's Workstyle project, *Flexible Working*, May.

BROWN, D. and EMMOTT, M. (2003) Happy days, *People Management,* October 23. 16–17.

CHARTERED INSTITUTE OF PERSONNEL AND DEVELOPMENT (CIPD) (2003) *Survey: age, pensions and retirement.* London: CIPD.

CIPD (2005) *Survey: flexible working, impact and implementation.* London: CIPD.

CIPD/LOVELLS (2003) *A parent's right to ask.* October. London: CIPD.

CLUTTERBUCK, D. (2003) *Managing work–life balance.* London: CIPD.

COOPER, A. (2003) Crisis, what crisis? *People Management,* 6 March. 21.

COUSSEY, M. (2000) *Getting the right work–life balance,* CIPD Research Report. London: CIPD.

COWEY, M. (2000) *New Zealand Management.* 54–55.

CULLY, M., O'REILLY, A., WOODLAND, S. and DIX, G. (1999) *Britain at Work.* London: Routledge.

DAVENPORT, T. and PRUSSAK, L. (1998) *Working knowledge: How organisations manage what they know.* Boston: Harvard Business School Press.

DENBIGH, A. (2003) *The teleworking handbook.* London: A and C Black.

DRUCKER, P. (1998) *Harvard Business Review,* Vol. 25. 20–24.

EMPLOYMENT TRENDS (2004) Home is where the work is. *Employment Trends.*

ENFIELD ADVERTISER (1997) Council's own workforce face bankruptcy. *Enfield Advertiser*, 27 April. 10.

FELSTEAD, A., JEWSON, P. and WALTERS, S. (2003) *In work at home.* London: Routledge.

FLEXIBLE WORKING (2000) Teleworking at Baxter International, *Flexible Working,* October. 11–14.

FLORIDA, R. (2002) *The rise of the creative classes.* New York: Basic Books.

FOGARTY, N. (2002) Real business benefits. *Interim HR Today,* Autumn. 17.

GRATTON, L. (2003) Burning questions. *People Management,* 24 July. 20.

HAMMOND, D. (2002) It shouldn't happen to a vetting. *People Management,* 21 November. 32–36.

HAYDEN-SMITH, J. (2003) It's a family affair. *People Management,* 17 April. 21.

HEBSON, G., GRIMSHAW, D. and MARCHINGTON, M. (2003) PPPs and the changing public sector ethos. *Work, Employment and Society,* Vol. 17, 3 September. 481–501.

HOLROYD, K. (1999) NatWest banks on a working year. *Flexible Working,* September. 8–9.

HOMAN, G. (2000) Skills and competence-based pay, in R. THORPE and G. HOMAN (eds), *Strategic reward systems.* London: Financial Times.

INCOMES DATA SERVICES (IDS) (2000) *Temporary workers,* Study 689, May. London: IDS.

IDS (2002) *Annual hours,* Study 721, January. London: IDS.

IDS (2004a) *Annual hours,* Study 767, February. London: IDS.

IDS (2004b) *Work–life balance,* Study 768, February. London: IDS.

INSTITUTE OF PERSONNEL AND DEVELOPMENT (IPD) (1994) *People make the difference.* Position paper. London: IPD.

IRS (1995) A hard day's night. *IRS Employment Trends,* No. 576. 9–16.

JACQUES, R. and LYNCH, I. (2004) IBM Staff in offshore outsourcing protest. *Management Consultancy,* 28 April. 5–7.

JOHNSON, M. (1997) *Outsourcing... in brief.* London: Butterworth-Heinemann.

JOHNSON, R. (1999) Constructive surgery. *People Management,* 11 November. 44–46.

JOSEPH ROWNTREE FOUNDATION (1999) *Whose flexibility? The costs and benefits of 'non-standard' working arrangements and contractual relations.* York: York Publishing Services.

KESSLER, I., COYLE-SHAPIRO, J. and PURCELL, J. (1999) Outsourcing and the employee perspective. *Human Resource Management Journal,* Vol. 9, No. 2. 5–19.

KNELL, K. and SAVAGE, C. (2001) *Desperately seeking flexibility.* London: Industrial Society.

LABOUR FORCE SURVEY (2005) *Temporary employees (reasons for temporary working)* Table 13b. Accessed at www.statistics.gov.uk/STATBASE.

LABOUR MARKET TRENDS (2002) Working patterns. *Labour Market Trends,* October. 506.

LABOUR MARKET TRENDS (2003) Temporary employees. *Labour Market Trends,* April. 167–169.

LACITY, M., HIRSCHHEIM, R. and WILLCOCKS, L. (1994) Realizing outsourcing expectations. *Information Systems Management,* Fall. 7–18.

LEWIS, M. (2001) *Next: the future just happened,* New York: Norton.

LOCAL GOVERNMENT MANAGEMENT BOARD (LGMB) (1996) *CCT information service survey,* Report No. 14, December. London: LGMB.

LONSDALE, C. and COX, A. (1998) Falling in with the out crowd. *People Management,* 15 October. 52–55.

MAHONEY, C. (2002) Guide to work–life balance. *People Management,* 26 September.

MARSTON, E., LEARMOND-CRIQUI, J. and HOLT, P. (2003), Alternative medicine. *People Management*, 9 January. 19.

McCARTNEY, C. (2003) Address the balance, *People Management*, 28 August. 39.

MURRAY, B. and GERHART, B (1998) An empirical analysis of skill-based program and plant performance outcomes. *Academy of Management Journal*, Vol. 41, No. 1. 68–70.

NOLAN, P. (2001) *Willing Slaves? Employment in Britain in the 21st century.* Swindon: ESRC.

PEOPLE MANAGEMENT (2002) Guide to interim managers. Supplement, *People Management,* September. 12.

PEOPLE MANAGEMENT (2003) Call centre offshoring may damage firms. *People Management,* 4 December. 7.

PERSAUD, J. (2003) Keep the faithful. *People Management,* 12 June. 37.

PM ONLINE (2004) Making work–life balance work for the business: the experts' views. www.peoplemanagement.co.uk/pm/articles. Accessed April 04.

PICKARD, J. (1998) Externally yours. *People Management,* 23 July. 34–36.

RANA, E. (2002) The CEO who gave his bank balance, *People Management,* Supplement, Guide to work–life balance. 6–7.

REED MANAGED SERVICES (2002) *Managing outsourcing: managing the working life cycle.* London: Reed.

REILLY, P. and TAMKIN, P. (1996) *Outsourcing: a flexible option for the future?* Report no. 320. Brighton: Institute for Employment Studies.

RITZER, G. (1996) *The McDonaldisation of Society,* New York: Sage.

RODGERS, K. (2002) Perils of partnership. *Personnel Today,* 26 March. 28–29.

SCHLESINGER, L. and HESKETT, J. (1992) Breaking the cycle of failure in services, in C. Lovelock (ed.), *Managing services, marketing, operations and human resources,* New York: Prentice Hall International.

SIMMS, J. (2004) Home or away? *People Management,* 3 June. 35–39.

SMETHURST, S. (2003a) Pooling resources. *People Management,* 1 May. 28–30.

SMETHURST, S. (2003b) Cut to the quick. *Human Resources,* October. 6–9.

STREDWICK, J. (1997) Time on the line. *Flexible Working*, September. 23–24.

SUFF, P. (1998) Complements of the season. *Flexible Working*, July. 9–10.

TARPEY, L. (2004) Working at being happy. *Care and Health*, 5 February. 22–23.

TAYLOR, S. (2002) *People resourcing.* London: CIPD.

TRENEMAN, A. (2002) Cut your hours, keep your career. *The Times*, 24 September. 2–3.

UNIVERSITY OF SHEFFIELD (2004) *New strategies in IT outsourcing: major trends and global best practice.* Sheffield: University of Sheffield.

VAN DE VELDE, M. and VAN DE VELDE, P. (2003) Managing functional flexibility in a passenger transport firm. *Human Resource Management Journal*, Vol. 13, No. 4. 42–55.

WARNER, J. (2000) Knight patrol. *Flexible Working*, July. 10–11.

WHYTE, W. (1956) *The organisation man.* New York: Simon and Schuster.

WINTER, S. (1987) *Knowledge and competence as strategic assets,* New York: Harper and Row.

WOOLNOUGH, R. (2003) Child benefits. *People Management*, 4 December. 40–41.

WORKING FAMILIES (2003) *NHS Management Awards,* accessed at workingfamilies.org.uk April 2005.

WUSTEMANN, L. (1999a) Lloyds TSB: keeping its work options open. *Flexible Working*, September. 6–8

WUSTEMANN, L. (1999b) Just the ticket. *Flexible Working*, May. 12–13.

FURTHER INFORMATION AND CONTACTS

For more guidance on annualised hours and rostering systems, contact Working Time Solutions: ‹workingtime-solutions.com›.

More information on interim management is available in *People Management* (2002) (see above).

       IPD Locum Service: tel. 0181 263 3348.

Association of Temporary and Interim Services (ATIES), 36–38 Mortimer Street, London W1N 7RB. Tel. 0171 323 4300.

For details of the study of older employees downshifting:
LISSENBURGH, S and SMEATON, D. (2003) *The role of flexible employment for older workers.* London: Policy Studies Institute.

More information on TUPE can be found in
LEWIS, D. and SARGEANT, M. (2003) *Essentials of employment law.* London: CIPD.

A general book on outsourcing:
ALLERY, P. (2004) *Effective outsourcing; practices and procedures.* London: Lexis Nexis.

For the debate on outsourcing payroll see *People Management*, 25 February 1999, 48–49.

For a more detailed analysis of partnership and outsourcing in the public sector, see:
GRIMSHAW, D., VINCENT, S. and WILLMOTT, H. (2002) Going privately. *Public Administration*, Vol. 80, No. 3. 475–502.

For an extended case of outsourcing HR, see:
WUSTEMANN, L. (2003) Outsourcing HR at Novo Nordisk. *IRS Employment Review*, No. 787, 7 November. 19–21.

For work–life balance standards, contact Work Life Balance Consultancy (WLBC): ‹www.wlbc.ltd.uk›, tel. 01460 77713.

Investors in People: ‹www.iipuk.co.uk›.

EfWLB, ‹www.employersforwork-lifebalance.org.uk› has an online benchmarking tool which can provide a useful reference and advice point for businesses.

For a detailed study of work–life balance see: CENTRE FOR DIVERSITY POLICY RESEARCH (2005) *A guide to work–life balance and good practice at Oxford Brookes University.* Oxford: Oxford Brookes University.

Index